Literacy in Context

Language of
literary non-fiction

Grainne Nelson *with* **Ian Aspey**

With contributions from Lyn Ranson and Glenn Mascord

General editors   **Joan Ward** *and* **John O'Connor**
Literacy consultant **Lyn Ranson**
General consultant   **Frances Findlay**

CAMBRIDGE
UNIVERSITY PRESS

PUBLISHED BY THE PRESS SYNDICATE OF THE UNIVERSITY OF CAMBRIDGE
The Pitt Building, Trumpington Street, Cambridge, United Kingdom

CAMBRIDGE UNIVERSITY PRESS
The Edinburgh Building, Cambridge CB2 2RU, UK
40 West 20th Street, New York, NY 10011-4211, USA
10 Stamford Road, Oakleigh, VIC 3166, Australia
Ruiz de Alarcón 13, 28014 Madrid, Spain
Dock House, The Waterfront, Cape Town 8001, South Africa

http://www.cambridge.org

First published 2001

Printed in the United Kingdom at the University Press, Cambridge

Typeface Delima MT 10.5pt on 12.5pt leading *System* QuarkXPress®

A catalogue record for this book is available from the British Library

ISBN 0 521 80566 X paperback

Prepared for publication by Pentacor PLC

Cover photograph by Jess Stock

Illustrations by Brian Lee (pp. 62–63, 68–69)

ACKNOWLEDGEMENTS

Textual material Extract from *Boy* by Roald Dahl (pp. 8, 9) published by Jonathan Cape & Penguin Books, reprinted by permission of David Higham Associates Ltd; extract from *A Nurse at the Russian Front* (pp. 14, 15) by Florence Farmborough, published by Constable and Robinson Publishers, reprinted by permission of Constable & Robinson Publishing Ltd; extract from *The Story of Grace Darling* (pp. 26, 27) by Helen Cresswell published by Viking Kestrel, 1988 © Helen Cresswell 1988, reprinted by permission of Penguin Books Ltd; extract from *Bound Feet and Western Dress* (pp. 32, 33) © 1996 Pang-Mei Natasha Chang, published by Bantam, a division of Transworld Publishers, all rights reserved; extract from *Captain Scott's Diary* (pp. 38, 39) March 1912 South Polar Expedition, reprinted by permission of The British Library; extract from *Managing My Life* (pp. 44, 45) by Alex Ferguson, reproduced by permission of Hodder and Stoughton Ltd; *El Guerrouj on the verge of greatness* (pp. 50, 51) by Robert Philip from the *Daily Telegraph* September 2000, © Telegraph Group Ltd, reproduced with permission of the *Daily Telegraph*; extract from *Notes from a Small Island* by Bill Bryson, reproduced by permission of Transworld Publishers; extract from *Mutiny on the Bounty* (*Famous Names in Crime*) (pp. 62, 63) by Prudence Mumford, reproduced by permission of Hodder and Stoughton Ltd; extract from *Both Sides of the Bell* (p. 64) by R. W. Taylor, edited by Bignell/Taylor, published by Oliver and Boyd, reproduced with permission of Pearson Education Ltd; extract from *Anglesey Diary* (pp. 70–72) by Tony Robinson, reproduced by permission of Tony Robinson; extract from Newnes Encyclopedia 1951 (p. 73) reproduced by permission of Octopus Publishing Group (Philips).

Photographs Great War nurse (p. 15) by F. J. Mortimer, by permission of Hulton Getty; Man on the moon (pp. 20, 21) (PASAN/RBO) by permission of Camera Press Ltd, Buzz Aldrin (taken by Neil Armstrong) by permission of Paul Popper Ltd; waves (pp. 26, 27) by permission of Superstock; lily feet of a Chinese lady (p. 33) by permission of Paul Popper Ltd; Gerache Straits at full moon (pp. 38, 39) Peter Oxford by permission of Telegraph Colour Library; The Antarctic (p. 39) J. Chester by permission of Camera Press Ltd; pp. 44–45 Teddy Sheringham by Clive Mason, David Beckham by Ben Radford, Alex Ferguson by Kenny Ramsey, all reproduced by permission of Allsport UK Ltd; El Guerrouj (p. 50) by Glyn Kirk reproduced by permission of Actionplus; Blackpool (pp. 56, 57 and Anglesey (pp. 70–72) from Bill Meadows Picture Library, reproduced by permission of Bill Meadows.

Every effort has been made to trace copyright holders, but in some cases this has proved impossible. The publishers would be happy to hear from any copyright holder that has not been acknowledged.

Introduction

- Read a piece of text
- Read it again to discover what makes it special
- Check that you understand it
- Focus on key features
- Learn about the language features and practise using them
- Improve your spelling
- Plan and write your own similar piece
- Check it and redraft

Each unit in this book helps you to understand more about a particular kind of writing, learn about its language features and work towards your own piece of writing in a similar style.

Grammar, spelling and punctuation activities, based on the extract, will improve your language skills and take your writing to a higher level.

 **The book at a glance**

The texts

The extracts are based on the National Curriculum reading lists. Each part of the book contains units of extracts and activities at different levels to help you measure your progress.

Each unit includes these sections:

Purpose

This explains exactly what you will read, learn about and write.

Key features

These are the main points to note about the way the extract is written.

Language skills

These activities will improve your grammar, punctuation and spelling. They are all based on the extracts. They are organised using the Word, Sentence and Text Level Objectives of the *National Literacy Strategy Framework*.

Planning your own writing

This structured, step-by-step guide will help you to get started, use writing frames and then redraft and improve your work.

Teacher's Portfolio

This includes worksheets for more language practice, revision and homework. Self-assessment charts will help you to judge and record what level you have reached and to set your own targets for improvement.

Contents

Word	Spelling	Sentence	Text	Activities
• Vocabulary • Etymology	• *-ght* words	• Direct speech	• Metaphor	Produce a piece of autobiographical writing
• Adjectives • Adverbs	• Prefixes • Suffixes	• Semicolon • Passive/active verbs	• Imagery • Metaphor	Write a journal about your own life
• Apostrophe • Specialist vocabulary	• *ie* and *ei*	• Sensory language	• Structure	Write a report of an important event

• Specialist vocabulary • Adjectives	• *-ly* suffix	• Contrast • Colon	• Paragraphs	Write about a person whose job is dangerous
• Hyphen	• Suffixes	• Verb tenses • Imperatives	• First/third person • Direct/indirect (reported) speech	Compose a first-person account of a painful experience
• Euphemisms	• *ph/gh* pronounced as 'f'	• Ellipsis	• Word order	Write a diary of someone who endures harsh living conditions

Contents

Word	Spelling	Sentence	Text	Activities
• Types of nouns	• Breaking words into syllables	• Parenthesis	• Specialist vocabulary	Write the opening to your autobiography
• Apostrophes (possession)	• Silent letters	• Alliteration • Simile	• Quotation marks (single/double)	Create a news article profiling a person you admire
• Prepositions	• -ier suffix	• Length of sentences	• Reader/writer relationship • Statistics	Describe somewhere or something you dislike

• Abstract nouns	• Mnemonics	• Commas	• Chronology • Sentence types • Structure	Put together a chronological account of a true event
• Etymology	• eau pattern	• Rhetorical questions • Verb tenses	• Colloquial and formal language • Fact and opinion	Write two descriptions using different styles

Six strokes of the cane

1 ▷ Purpose

In this unit you will:
- read an extract from an autobiography
- learn about how the writer makes a scene come alive
- write your own piece of autobiography

➤➤ **Subject links:** *PSHE, citizenship*

2 ▷ Autobiography

Boy

'Enter!'

I turned the knob and went into this large square room with bookshelves and easy chairs and the gigantic desk topped in red leather straddling the far corner. The Headmaster was sitting behind the desk. 'What have you got to say for yourself?' he asked me and the white shark's teeth flashed dangerously between his lips. 5

'I didn't lie, sir,' I said. 'I promise I didn't. And I wasn't trying to cheat.'

'Captain Hardcastle says you were doing both,' the Headmaster said. 'Are you calling Captain Hardcastle a liar?' 10

'No sir. Oh no, sir.'

'I wouldn't if I were you.'

'I had broken my nib, sir, and I was asking Dobson if he could lend me another.'

'That is not what Captain Hardcastle says. He says you were asking for help with your essay.' 15

'Oh no, sir, I wasn't. I was a long way away from Captain Hardcastle and I was only whispering. I don't think he could have heard what I said, sir.'

'So you are calling him a liar.' 20

'Oh no, sir! No, sir! I would never do that!'...

'For talking in Prep,' the Headmaster went on, 'for trying to cheat and for lying, I am going to give you six strokes of the cane.'

He rose from his desk and crossed over to the corner cupboard on the opposite side of the study. He reached up and took from the top of it three very thin yellow canes, each with the bent-over handle at one end. For a few seconds, he held them in his hands, examining them 25

with some care, then he selected one and replaced the other two on
top of the cupboard.

'Bend over.' 30

I was frightened of that cane. There is no small boy in the world
who wouldn't be. It wasn't simply an instrument for beating you. It
was a weapon for wounding. It lacerated the skin. It caused severe
black and scarlet bruising that took three weeks to disappear, and all
the time during those three weeks, you could feel your heart beating 35
along the wounds.

I tried once more, my voice slightly hysterical now. 'I didn't do it,
sir! I swear I'm telling the truth!'

'Be quiet and bend over! Over there! And touch your toes!'

Very slowly, I bent over. Then I shut my eyes and braced myself 40
for the first stroke.

Crack! It was like a rifle shot! With a very hard stroke of a cane
on one's buttocks, the time lag before you feel any pain is about four
seconds. Thus, the experienced caner will always pause between
strokes to allow the agony to reach its peak. 45

So for a few seconds after the first crack I felt virtually nothing.
Then suddenly came the frightful, searing, agonising, unbearable,
burning across the buttocks, and as it reached its highest and most
excruciating point, the second crack came down. I clutched hold of
my ankles as tight as I could and I bit into my lower lip. I was 50
determined not to make a sound, for that would only give the
executioner greater satisfaction.

Crack!.....Five seconds pause.

Crack!.....Another pause.

Crack!.....And another pause. 55

I was counting the strokes, and as the sixth one hit me, I knew
I was going to survive in silence.

'That will do,' the voice behind me said.

I did not look at the Headmaster as I hopped across the thick red
carpet towards the door. The door was closed, so for a couple of 60
seconds I had to let go of my bottom with one hand to turn the
door knob. Then I was out and
hopping around in the hallway
of the inner sanctum.

Roald Dahl

3 Key features

The writer:

- uses direct speech to make
  the characters come alive
- uses metaphors and vivid
  vocabulary to help the reader
  imagine the scene

- What had happened just before the incident described here?
- What impressions do you have of the kind of school the writer attends?
- Why do you think the boy was determined to *survive in silence*?

4 > Language skills

Word

Vocabulary is the choice of words used by a writer.

In this extract, Roald Dahl uses precise and vivid vocabulary to help the reader to imagine the scene.

❶ Copy this list of words from the text and match them to the list of definitions. Try to work out the correct meaning and use the dictionary to check your answers. The first one has been done for you.

straddling	intense pain
instrument	sitting or standing across something
hysterical	skilled
braced	tool
experienced	burning
agony	out of control
searing	steadied

Etymology is the history of a particular word, including the language it came from and its original meaning.

In this extract, the writer uses the phrase *the inner sanctum* to describe the Headmaster's study. The word *sanctum* comes from the Latin root which means a *sacred* or *holy place*.

Here are ten other common Latin roots:

bene	= good		spectare	= to look
audio	= I hear		fractus	= break
terra	= land		annus	= year
aqua	= water		scribo	= I write
centum	= one hundred		signum	= sign

❷ Write down these ten English words. Next to each, write the Latin word from the list which is related to it. Then write the meaning of the Latin word.

spectator	territory
century	audience
anniversary	aquarium
beneficial	fracture
signature	scripture

Spelling

In the extract, Roald Dahl describes the pain as *frightful*. The word *frightful* contains the letters *-ght* which are pronounced as 't'.

❶ Find and write down three other words in the extract which also use this string of letters.

❷ Make a list of all the other words you can think of which contain this string of letters.

Here are two to start your list:

caught
bright

Sentence

In **direct speech** a writer shows a character's exact words, using speech punctuation.

Notice how:

- the spoken sentence always begins with a capital letter
- the writer begins a new paragraph for each speaker
- he/she uses speech marks (inverted commas) to mark spoken words.
- punctuation marks such as the comma, full stop and question mark are placed inside the speech marks

1 Write out the following paragraph using words and phrases from this list to fill in the gaps:

comma	speech marks
spoken	inside
capital letter	paragraphs

Writers use _____ to indicate that a character in the story is speaking. The words which are _____ the speech marks are the words which are actually _____ . The spoken sentence must always begin with a _____ .
If you add the speaker's name to the end of a spoken sentence, separate the two by using a _____ .

Text

A **metaphor** is a way of comparing things without using the words *like* or *as*, where the writer writes about something as if it were really something else.

Metaphors provide original and fresh ways of describing something, which helps the reader to imagine it.

The white shark's teeth flashed dangerously between his lips...

Here, the Headmaster's teeth are described as though they were *actually* sharks' teeth rather than just like sharks' teeth.

1 Think about sharks' teeth. Write down what they look like and what they do.

2 Draw a cartoon picture of a shark with big, sharp, vicious teeth. Beside it, draw a cartoon picture of the Headmaster with the same teeth.

3 Write your impression of the Headmaster from being told his teeth were *shark's teeth*.

4 Make a list of ten common metaphors which are used to describe aspects of the human body. Here are a few:

the apple of her eye
heartbroken
stars in her eyes
butterflies in my stomach
ears burning
frog in my throat

5 ▷ Planning your own writing

Write about a time when you have been punished unfairly for something you did not do. In your writing, try to describe the pain you felt and the sense of anger at being unfairly treated. Read the extract again before you begin, to remind you of how the author wrote about his own experience.

▷▷ STARTING POINTS

You could write about being wrongly accused of:

- shoplifting

- breaking something which was valuable

- treating a younger brother or sister badly

- playing truant or not doing a key piece of work

- telling a lie

Here is a list of words and phrases which might help you:

summoned
anticipation
sense of dread
butterflies in my stomach
heart beating
palms sweating
hoarse whisper
stuttering
faltering steps
anxiety
trepidation
accusing
overwhelmed by anger
outrage
protest

▷▷ CLUES FOR SUCCESS

- Begin your account by writing about where you were and what you were doing when you were first accused.

- Plan how you are going to present your account in a way that is clear, interesting and which will express your feelings.

- Choose vivid vocabulary which shows your thoughts and feelings.

- Use direct speech to reproduce what was said and to make the characters come alive.

- Describe the characters clearly, using metaphors to create pictures of their appearance.

▷▷ REDRAFTING AND IMPROVING

- Is your vocabulary interesting and lively? Have you used any metaphors in your writing?

- Does it have realistic speech which makes the scene come alive? Have you used speech marks correctly?

- Have you described the other people and written about how you felt?

- Is your writing presented in sentences and paragraphs to make it easy to understand?

- Are there any corrections needed to spelling?

WRITING FRAMES

Writing frame A

Begin by writing what happened when you were first accused. Where were you?
How did you know you were in trouble? You might begin like this:

My brother, Sam, just loves it when I'm in trouble. His sneaky freckled face lights up with pleasure and he can hardly stop laughing. That's why I knew I was in for it when he appeared in my bedroom.

'Mum wants you – now!' he announced with a wide grin. 'In the kitchen.'

Mum's face was like thunder. She stood stiffly by the sink, tapping the draining board angrily with her long nails. The sound was horribly like the sound of a firing squad. When I appeared at the door, she turned to face me, eyes glinting.

'Explain yourself!' she snapped. Her voice was thunderous.

How did you feel? Did you know what the problem was? What happened next?
Write about the conversation. What were you accused of? How did you feel?

I could not believe it! How could she believe that I would do such a thing? The unfairness of it took my breath away.

'But I didn't...' I began. My voice wobbled.

I tried again. 'It's not fair...'

'Don't try to make excuses,' Mum snarled. 'You'll just make it worse!'

How did the incident end? How were you punished and how did you feel afterwards?

'Don't argue with me! I have told you what will happen and that's that!'

With these words, Mum stormed out of the

kitchen, banging the door angrily behind her. In the silence that followed, I tried to make sense of it. I was overwhelmed by anger and outrage.

Writing frame B

I cannot believe it!
I will never forget the feeling when...
Before I knew it...
How could I make anyone believe me after I had...
I had to act now...
When it was all over...

6 ▷ Looking back

- Choosing **vocabulary** with care can help you to express ideas clearly and make your writing more interesting.

- Writers use **metaphors** to create original and vivid images.

- Using **direct speech** makes characters come alive and creates interest for your readers.

Nurse at war

1 ▶ Purpose

In this unit you will:
- read extracts from a journal
- understand the features of a journal
- write about your own experiences in a journal

▶▶ **Subject links:** *PSHE, history*

2 ▶ Journal

A Nurse at the Russian Front

28 May (1916) Buchach

An urgent message reached us: 'Prepare for burnt soldiers.' Laconic wording, but elaborated in some detail by the staff messenger. A disastrous fire had gutted a wine-cellar; several soldiers had been burnt to death; some were being brought for instant treatment. It seems that the men of the 101st Permski regiment had that day

5   marched through Buchach, singing lustily, on their way into reserve. During the evening, several had gone on a tour of exploration. They found a distillery in which cases of alcohol were still stored. They drank their fill and then, inebriated and elated, turned on the taps. But someone must have struck a match, for the cellar was suddenly swept with fierce flames. About a dozen men perished on the spot; others

10   crawled out, but collapsed and died soon afterwards. Only two of them were able to stand and they were brought to us.

    They came, both of them, *walking*: two naked red figures! Their clothes had been burnt off their bodies. They stood side by side in the large barn which we had converted into a dressing station, raw from head to foot. Injections were immediately

15   ordered, but we could find no skin and had to put the needle straight into the flesh. Their arms were hanging stiffly at their sides and from the finger-tips of the men were suspended what looked like leather gloves; these we were told to cut off which we did with surgical scissors. They were the skin of the hand and fingers which had peeled off and was hanging from the raw flesh of the fingertips. Then we showered

20   them with bicarbonate of soda and swathed their poor burnt bodies with layers of cotton wool and surgical lint. We laid them down upon straw in an adjoining shed. In an hour or two, the cotton wool was completely saturated, but we could help them

25 no further save with oft-repeated injections of morphia which, we prayed, would deaden their sufferings. They died, both of them, before morning, and neither of them had spoken a single word! I don't think that anything which I had ever seen touched me more keenly.

Sunday 31 July (1916) Monasterzhiska

We were still surrounded by the gruesome remains of the recent conflict. Not far from our tent, there was a slight incline with a couple of dug-outs; a dead man was lying near them, half-buried in the piled earth thrown up by a shell... To our right was a plain; there, too, was a litter of bombs, hand-grenades, cartridges, rifles, spades, pickaxes, gas-masks, shells exploded and unexploded...

35 On another part of the plain, many bodies were strewn; all in different attitudes — many on knees; others lying prone, with arms flung out; some had fallen head-first and buried their head in the soil; while still others were lying on their side, arms crossed as though they had found time to compose themselves before Death had released them from their sufferings.

40 ... It seemed that some effort had been made to bury the dead, for to the north of that village a pit had been dug, in which some fifty soldiers had been deposited; the pit had not yet been filled in and here too the sight and smell of the decaying
45 bodies were terrible. We left this gloomy place...

Florence Farmborough

3 Key features

The writer:
- uses adjectives and adverbs to make her writing powerful
- uses a range of punctuation, including the semicolon
- uses passive verb forms
- uses the personal pronouns *I* and *We* because it is a personal record
- uses images and metaphor to describe vividly what she has seen

- What impression do you get of the conditions suffered by the soldiers?
- What aspects of this journal make you feel pity?
- How many weapons of war are mentioned in the text?

4 ⟩ Language skills

Word

Adverbs can give more information about verbs by telling you how actions were done.

Adjectives are words which describe or give more information about nouns or pronouns.

❶ Find the paragraph which begins *They came, both of them...* List all the adjectives and adverbs. Start your lists like this:

Adjectives   **Adverbs**
naked   *immediately*

❷ From your lists, select three adjectives and three adverbs which have added to your understanding. For each word, write down what impact this word has on you. Your comment might be like this:

I think the adjective 'naked' is powerful because it makes me realise how badly injured they were. Their clothes were burned off their bodies. I also feel sorry for them because they were walking naked in front of other people. They were in such pain that they did not feel embarrassed.

Spelling

A **prefix** is a group of letters added to the start of a word to change its meaning or to create a new word

dis + satisfaction makes *dissatisfaction*, the opposite of satisfaction

A **suffix** is a letter or group of letters added to the end of a word to change its meaning or to create a new word.

peace + full makes *peaceful* (note the change to the spelling of *full* when used as a suffix)

Look at these words from the passage:

Adjoining   suddenly   perished

They are all formed by adding a *prefix* or a *suffix* to a *root word*.

Adjoining is made up in this way
Ad – join – ing

The root word is *join*. The prefix is *ad-*. The suffix is *-ing*.

❶ Make three columns, headed *Prefix, Root, Suffix*. Write down the other words by breaking them down and listing the parts in the right column. Each word might have a prefix or a suffix or both.

Sentence

The **semicolon (;)** can be used to provide a stronger break in a sentence than a comma. It can also be used to separate longer items in a list.

In peace, sons bury their fathers;
in war, fathers bury their sons.

❶ In the extract, find and write down two more examples of where the writer uses the semicolon to mark pauses within sentences.

❷ In the entry of 31 July, find and write down an example of where the writer uses the semicolon to separate items of a list.

The **active** form of a verb is where the subject carries out the action.

The **passive** form of a verb is where the subject is on the receiving end of the action.

John kicked the ball. (Active)
The ball was kicked by John. (Passive)

❸ Write five sentences using active verbs. Then turn each of your active sentences into the passive, e.g.

Rifat borrowed my pen (active) ➜
My pen was borrowed by Rifat
(passive).

Text

An **image** is a vivid picture in words created by a writer to help us to imagine what is being described.

...from the fingertips of the men were suspended what looked like leather gloves.

Here, the writer suggests the dark colour of leather gloves and their smooth, hide-like texture.

A **metaphor** is a way of comparing one thing to another, in which the writer creates an image in the reader's mind without using the words *like* or *as*.

A disastrous fire had gutted a cellar...

Here the word *gutted* is used metaphorically. Its dictionary meaning is *to remove or destroy the internal organs*. It is often used to describe cleaning a fish, but it also has a suggestion of violence. Here, the cellar has not been emptied of its contents but the fire has destroyed them. It is a more powerful way of saying *The fire had destroyed the cellar*.

❶ Write a descriptive paragraph of a fire, using at least two images and two metaphors to make your description powerful. You could begin like this:

The fire was like a wild animal, devouring everything in its path...

5 Planning your own writing

Write a journal about your own life. You may not be able to report dramatic or exciting events like Nurse Farmborough, but your life is interesting too. Imagine that your diary will be discovered and read in a hundred years time. What would future readers learn about you, your life and the way you feel about issues that are important to you? Write an entry for today and one for tomorrow.

▷▷ CLUES FOR SUCCESS

- Use adjectives and adverbs to make your writing more descriptive.

- Use the personal pronoun *I* when writing about yourself.

- Use the semicolon to divide longer sentences and to separate longer items in a list.

- Make your writing vivid by using images and metaphors.

- Select your events carefully.

▷▷ STARTING POINTS

Write about:

- the people you meet and your feelings about them

- the things which happen to you, however ordinary they might seem

- your thoughts about your life

- your views about important issues which affect your life

September 2001   WEEK 36

6 *Thursday*
(249-116)

WRITING FRAMES

Use one of these writing frames to get you started.

Writing frame A

Monday 8 March

When I woke up today, I felt really happy because...

I met Sam on the way to school and we decided to...

School was pretty normal except for...

At lunchtime we...

I can't stand...

After school was over, I went...

The best part was when...

In the evening, I...

When I thought about it later, I decided that...

Writing frame B

Monday 8 March

I woke up in a vile temper, simmering with resentment at the prospect of...

Things went from bad to worse when I met Sam, who told me...

At school...

The day began to improve when...

I'm beginning to think that...

The family has been trying to help in its own special way. The result is...

Anyway, I've now decided that...

REDRAFTING AND IMPROVING

- Have you used first person pronouns and dated your entries?
- Have you written in a way that is interesting to read, using images and metaphors?
- Is your writing presented in sentences and paragraphs? Have you used the semicolon?
- Have you expressed your feelings about your life?

6 ▷ Looking back

- **Images** and **metaphors** are used by writers to make their writing fresh and original.
- The **semicolon** is a punctuation mark used to mark pauses in a sentence in a stronger way than a comma, and sometimes to separate items in a list.
- Writers use **passive verb** forms to show the effects of verbs and to emphasise the action, not the subject.

One giant leap

1 ▶ Purpose

In this unit you will:
- read a report of an important event
- learn how to write a report
- write a piece of reportage of your own

▶▶ **Subject links:** *science, history, geography*

2 ▶ Reportage

The first men on the moon

Apollo II, carrying Neil Armstrong, Lieutenant-Colonel Michael Collins and Colonel Edwin Aldrin, was launched on 16 July. At 3.56 BST on 21 July, Armstrong stepped off the ladder of lunar landing vehicle Eagle onto the moon.

Neil Armstrong The most dramatic recollections I had were the sights themselves. Of all the most spectacular views we had, the most impressive to me was on the way to the moon, when we flew across its shadow. We were still thousands of miles away, but close enough so that the moon almost filled our
5 circular window. It was eclipsing the sun, from our position, and the corona of the sun was visible around the limb of the moon as a gigantic lens-shaped or saucer-shaped light, stretching out to several lunar diameters. It was magnificent, but the moon was even more so. We were in its shadow, so there was no part of it illuminated by the sun. It was illuminated only by earthshine.
10 It made the moon appear blue-grey, and the entire scene looked decidedly three-dimensional.

I was really aware, visually aware, that the moon was in fact a sphere, not a disc. It seemed almost as if it were showing us its roundness, its similarity in shape to our earth, in a sort of welcome. I was sure that it would be a
15 hospitable host. It had been awaiting its first visitors for a long time...

(After touchdown)   The sky is black, you know. It's a very dark sky. But it still seemed more like daylight than darkness as we looked out the window. It's a peculiar thing, but the surface looked very warm and inviting. It was the sort of situation in which you felt like going out there in nothing but a swimming suit to get a little sun. From the cockpit, the surface seemed to be tan. It's hard to account for that, because later when I held this material in my hand, it wasn't tan at all. It was black, grey and so on. It's some kind of lighting effect, but out of the window, the surface looks much more like light desert sand than black sand.

20

Edwin E Aldrin *(On the moon)*   The blue colour of my boot has completely disappeared now into this – still don't know exactly what colour to describe this other than greyish-cocoa colour. It appears to be covering most of the lighter part of my boot... very fine particles...

25

Odour is very subjective, but to me there was a distinct smell to the lunar material – pungent, like gunpowder or spent cap-pistol caps. We carted a fair amount of lunar dust back inside the vehicle with us, either on our suits and boots or in the conveyor system we used to get boxes and equipment back inside. We did notice the odour straight away.

30

35

David Thompson

3 ❯ **Key features**

In this text the writer:
- structures his material by using the words of eye-witnesses
- uses the senses to describe
- uses specialist vocabulary

- What nationality were Armstrong and Aldrin?
- What was unusual about the moon's surface?
- What unusual feeling did they have to get used to?

4 > Language skills

Word

The **apostrophe** (') is a punctuation mark with two uses:

- to show that one or more letters has been missed out

    It's a very dark sky...

Here the letter *i* has been missed out from the word *is* so that *It is* becomes *It's*.

- to show possession or ownership

    the moon's atmosphere

In this example the *'s* has been added to the word *moon* to show that the moon is the owner of the atmosphere.

❶ Reread the extract and note where the apostrophe has been used for shortening words.

❷ The following expressions use the apostrophe in place of missing letters. Write them down in a column and then write the expression in full. The first has been done for you.

I'm	= I am	*we're*
you're		*they're*
isn't		*wasn't*
who's		*hasn't*
you've		*weren't*
wouldn't		*that's*

Specialist vocabulary is the special words and phrases used by particular groups of people who share the same job or interest.

❸ In the moon landing extract there are several words which are difficult to understand.

Use a dictionary to check the meanings of these words and make a list of them and their meanings.

eclipsing (check *eclipse*)	*corona*
lunar	*illuminated*
sphere	*disc*
hospitable	*cockpit*
tan	*particles*
subjective	*pungent*

Spelling

When *ie* is used, it usually gives a sound which rhymes with *believe*.

The vowel combination *ei* can be pronounced in more than one way. For example, for the word *either*, some people say EE-ther and some say EYE-ther.

❶ The following *ei* words appear in the extract:

either neither seismic kaleidoscope

Write a short paragraph which includes these four words. Underline the letters *ei* in each word to help you remember the vowel pattern.

Sentence

Sensory language is where a writer refers to the five senses of sight, hearing, smell, taste and touch. Writers use the senses to develop and strengthen their descriptions.

1 Pick out five places where the witnesses refer to what they saw. Here is one to get you started:

> *...the corona of the sun was visible around the limb of the moon (sight)*

2 Which of the senses is being referred to in these extracts? Answer by copying out and completing the table.

Quote	Sense
The sky is black	
very fine particles	
pungent, like gunpowder	
It was illuminated only by earthshine.	

3 Write a paragraph to describe your favourite room, referring to the senses in your writing. You could use this model to give you ideas.

> *As I sit here, I can hear... I look around and see... From the kitchen, I can smell ...The air is cold on my face as I look through the open window. Outside,...*

Text

The **structure** of a text is the way it is put together in paragraphs.

In this piece of reportage, two of the astronauts remember their moon walk. Their words are eyewitness statements of what they saw and felt.

1 Here are summaries of what they say. Rearrange and write down the summaries in the order in which they occur in the extract.

- Aldrin remembers the distinctive smell of the moon.
- Armstrong comments on the shape of the moon.
- Armstrong describes his most vivid memory.
- Armstrong describes the colour and light on the moon.
- Aldrin describes the moondust.

2 Why did the author use two witnesses instead of just one? Write down three advantages of using the words of two different witnesses. Think about:

- points of view
- noticing different details
- supporting one another's statements by agreement

5 ▷ Planning your own writing

Write a report of an important event. It could be something from history or a famous occasion or just something from your own life. Include some eyewitness memories, similar to those used in the extract.

▶ STARTING POINTS

You could write about:

- an important family occasion like a birth, marriage, or other celebration

- a local or national event, like the Year 2000 celebrations or a town festival or carnival

- a pop concert, show, circus or other form of entertainment

- a big sporting event, like a cup final. You could get eyewitness views from people with contrasting opinions, in order to make your report more interesting. It could be an event of widespread importance, like an international match, or more local in interest, like a school game.

▶ CLUES FOR SUCCESS

- Begin by writing a brief factual paragraph, giving dates, names and other details. Give a very brief note of what is being reported on, for your reader to understand the background.

- Decide who your witnesses are. Limit the number to two and decide exactly what each will describe. Remember to include their reactions and feelings.

- Make a list of specialist vocabulary you might need to describe the event.

- Refer to the senses to give a vivid and detailed description.

WRITING FRAMES

Use one of these writing frames to help you.

Writing frame A

On the 22 April 2000, Lorna Downs and James Taylor were married.

Lorna: The first sight that I saw this morning was the locket James gave me last night. It glowed with a friendly radiance, reminding me...

Grace, her mother: By eleven, the flowers had arrived and the whole house seemed filled with the sweet scent of roses and freesia...

Writing frame B

July 30, 1966, Wembley. England had beaten Portugal to reach the final of the World Cup and a chance to meet their old rivals, Germany. Watching the match were Adrian Ward, a fervent England supporter, and Claus von Brun, who travelled from Munich to see the match.

Adrian: I will never forget the sight of Moore leading the red-shirted England team onto the pitch to make footballing history...

Claus: When Haller scored in the 13th minute, I thought my heart would burst with pride...

 REDRAFTING AND IMPROVING

- Is it clear who the witnesses are? Will the reader understand what their role was at the event?
- Have you used specialist vocabulary to make your writing convincing? Have you referred to the senses in your descriptions?
- Do your witnesses give a convincing account of their feelings and reactions?

6 ▷ Looking back

- **Specialist vocabulary** is used to make descriptions convincing and realistic.
- Using eyewitness statements to help **structure**, the writing adds interest and allows the author to show different points of view.
- Using **sensory language** allows writers to describe in a more intense way.

A daring rescue

1 ▶ **Purpose**

In this unit you will:
- read an extract from a biography
- learn how a writer creates a sense of danger
- write your own account of an exciting and dangerous event

▶▶ **Subject links:** *history, PSHE*

2 ▶ **Biography**

Grace Darling

On 7 September 1838, the Forfarshire *was wrecked on the dangerous rocks known as the Harcars in the middle of a violent storm. Grace Darling and her father, the local lighthouse keeper, bravely rowed out to the rocks and rescued passengers and crew who faced certain death.*

The Harcars lay only three hundred yards away, tantalisingly close. But to reach them, the Darlings had to row a mile, in the lee of the Blue Caps. All that long journey they were blinded by driving rain yet knew they were steering through treacherous rocks that might at any moment overturn them. Although it was past dawn it was still so dark it might have been the end ⁵ of the world.

The coble needed three men to row her in rough seas, and these were seas beyond imagination. Grace, with her slender wrists, had to pull on the heavy oar to match her father. Perhaps she did not have time to feel terror, to dread her own death by drowning. 10

When at last they drew near to the reef, the wreck loomed above them, a huge shape in the mist. Now they could see the people clinging for dear life on the rock, while the great clouds of spray broke over them.

Above the roar of wind and surf they heard a man's cry:

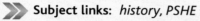 'For the Lord's sake, there's a lassie coming!' → Speech - 15
expressive
and then
an exclamation
mark
→ Shows emotion

26

Mr Darling saw at once that there were too many survivors to take off at once. A second trip, equally hazardous, would have to be made. The frantic people were now shouting and screaming, scrambling to reach the coble first. All but the still figure of a man lying on the gleaming rock, and two small shapes lying limply in their mother's arms. The Dawson children were dead.   20

Mr Darling acted swiftly. He knew he could not take all the howling and pleading survivors at once. Somehow he must reason with them. With the next high wave he himself leapt out on to the rock. Grace was left alone in the coble.

As an old man, Mr Darling said that those had been the worst moments of his life, when he had to leave his daughter all alone in the boat, frail as a   25
matchstick in those violent waves.

Grace's own heart stopped as she saw her father leap. She hardly believed her eyes. Now the lives of all of them depended on her. She clutched at her father's oar before it could be washed away. She knew what she must do to keep the coble off the rocks, or from being swept away altogether.   30

Those minutes when Grace, a tiny figure in her drenched clothes and bonnet, held the coble alone, were the longest of her life. She gasped as wave after wave struck the rocks, pitching the boat and blinding her with icy spray. All the time she held tightly on to both oars and desperately rowed backwards and forwards as quickly as possible, to keep the coble steady.   35

Her father swiftly selected the first boatload – a woman, a sick man and three of the crew. Grace pulled in the boat as close as she dared. Mrs. Dawson, moaning and pleading to be left with her children, was lifted in, then the injured man. The others waist-high in water, struggled aboard. Grace gave her oar to one of the sailors, and the dangerous trip back to the lighthouse began...   40

Helen Cresswell

3 > Key features

The writer:

- uses short paragraphs to emphasise the speed of events
- describes details of the danger to build a sense of suspense
- chooses appropriate vocabulary to describe the incident
- shows what is happening from several points of view

H/W 02/10/18.

- How many people were rescued?
- How do you know the survivors were shocked by the incident?
- Name three qualities shown by Grace in this extract.   PEA
  (with examples)

27

4 Language skills

Word

Specialist vocabulary is the special words and phrases used by particular groups of people who share the same job or interest.

❶ Use the passage to help you to match the seafaring words to the correct meaning. The first one has been done for you.

reef → throwing
coble → a ridge of rock
pitching   white foam of waves
surf   shower of water
lee   remains of a
    damaged ship
spray   sheltered side
wreck   small boat

An **adjective** is a word which describes somebody or something. Adjectives help to give more information about a noun or pronoun.

❷ Find the noun which is described by each of these adjectives. Fill in the blanks and underline the adjective. The first one has been done for you.

<u>treacherous</u> rocks
driving _____
huge _____
rough _____
long _____
howling and pleading
_____
frantic _____
drenched _____
high _____

Spelling

The **suffix -ly** can be added to some adjectives to make adverbs. Adverbs describe how actions are performed.

In the extract, the bodies of the dead children are lying *limply*. *Limply* is made from the adjective *limp* and the suffix *-ly*. Note that the *-ly* suffix has been added to whole words without changing them.

❶ Find six examples from the text where adverbs have been created by adding *-ly* to an adjective. Make two columns with the headings *Adjectives* and *Adverbs*. Write the adjectives in the first column, and then put the adverb which comes from it in the second.

If the adjective ends in the letter *-y*, change the *-y* to *-i* before adding the suffix *-ly* – for example, *icy + ly = icily*.

❷ Add the suffix *-ly* to these adjectives to make them into adverbs:

easy   gloomy   fussy
lucky   happy   funny

Sentence

A **contrast** is a clear and striking difference between two things.

Writers often use contrasts to create a dramatic effect.

Grace, with her slender wrists, had to pull on the heavy oar...

1 Here are some details from the extract. Copy and complete them by writing down the contrasting detail.

The frantic people were now shouting and screaming, scrambling to reach the coble first.

...he had to leave his daughter all alone, frail as a matchstick...

2 Write three sentences of your own which use contrasting detail to create a dramatic effect. For example:

Against the towering TV screens, the figure of the lead singer looked tiny and insignificant.

The **colon** can be used show that there is something else to follow in the sentence.

Above the roar of wind and surf they heard a man's cry:

'For the Lord's sake, there's a lassie coming!'

3 Write out the sentence below, using a colon in the correct place.

Winston Churchill said 'Never in the field of human conflict was so much owed by so many to so few.'

Text

The **structure** of a text is the way it is put together in **paragraphs**.

In this extract, the paragraphs show a) the sequence of events and b) the different points of view of the events.

1 Look at the paragraph beginning *Mr Darling acted swiftly.* The account in this paragraph is written from a particular person's point of view. Which person is it? How do you know? Write your answer by completing the following sentence:

This paragraph is written from the viewpoint of ————. I know this because ————.

2 Look at the last sentence *Grace was left alone in the coble.* Explain in writing how the writer has made us feel suspense. Think about the specific dangers and threats faced by Grace at this moment.

3 Sometimes a writer switches from one person's point of view to another's to make the account more dramatic or to add to the suspense. Find the most obvious place where Mr Darling's viewpoint switches to Grace's. In writing, explain how the writer makes it clear that the viewpoint has changed.

5 ▷ Planning your own writing

Write a chapter from a biography of a person whose job is dangerous. In your writing, describe an incident which was dangerous and exciting. Try to show the dangers faced by the characters, just as Grace faced danger in helping her father.

▷▷ STARTING POINT

- Decide on the subject of your writing – a police officer, fire officer, mountain rescuer, soldier, paramedic, miner, etc.

- Think about TV programmes you have seen which re-enact dramatic and dangerous incidents.

- Choose the specific incident you are going to write about.

- Plan how you will begin and end your writing.

▷▷ CLUES FOR SUCCESS

- Make a list of adjectives you might use to create a sense of danger.

- Set the scene carefully.

- Use short paragraphs and use contrast for a dramatic effect.

- Show different points of view to create a feeling of suspense.

▷▷ REDRAFTING AND IMPROVING

- With a partner, read each other's work and write a brief comment on what was good about it. If there was anything you did not understand, write a brief note about that, too.

- Reread your writing. Check that you have made it exciting. Make sure the paragraphs are short, to create a feeling of pace and action. Use adverbs and adjectives to make the scene come alive.

- Ask yourself if you have shown the dangers of the work.

- Make any corrections and changes you think are needed and then make or print a best copy.

WRITING FRAME

Set the scene. Use details to make the place come alive for your reader.	The derelict house was alight. Flames licked around empty window frames and curled up the brick walls...
Bring on your hero or heroine!	A loud siren wailed and a red fire engine squealed to a stop in the street outside. Sam leaped down, closely followed by...
Some dialogue to show reactions of onlookers.	'For God's sake! Help him! My son's in there,' shrieked an elderly man frantically, tears streaming down his lined cheeks.
Action stations!	Sam uncoiled the long, glistening hosepipe and hooked it to a nearby standpipe. Within seconds, a graceful arc of water spurted out and was directed at the flames...
More heroics.	Sam put on a mask. 'I'm going in! Cover me!'
How does it end?	Through the clouds of smoke and sooty flames, a bent figure emerged. It was carrying what looked like a huge, shapeless sack...

6 > Looking back

- **Paragraph structure** helps to get across the speed and sequence of events.
- Dramatic effects can be achieved by using **contrasting detail** and carefully chosen **adjectives**.
- Interest and drama can be added by showing different **viewpoints** of the same events.
- Writers use **specialist vocabulary** to make their writing true to life and convincing.

A child's torment

1 ▷ **Purpose**

In this unit you will:
- read a biographical account
- discover how the writer helps you to share her pain
- write a personal account

▶▶ **Subject links:** *PSHE, citizenship, history*

2 ▷ **Autobiography**

Bound Feet and Western Dress

In this extract, Natasha Chang tells us about the ancient Chinese custom of binding the feet of young girls to make their feet small, a sign of great beauty in a woman.

How small, how beautiful, then, the bound foot. Give me your hand so you might see how it is done, how the toes of the feet are taught to curve gently around the sole of the foot until they touch your heel. Imagine your palm as the sole and your fingers as the toes. See how your fingers
5 in your palm make a loose fist in the shape of a new moon?

That is the bound foot – you end up walking on your heels and the knuckles of your toes – and if it is perfectly formed, you can slide three fingers into the niche between the toes and the heels.   gap, opening

My mother had three-inch feet that she wrapped in fresh bandages every
10 morning and bathed in perfumed water in the evening. When she walked, stiff-legged and sway-hipped, the tips of her embroidered slippers peeped out, first one and then the other, from the edge of her robe. My **amah**, who came   servant from the countryside and whose feet were big like a man's, said if I were good I would grow up to be like my mother, pale and beautiful like one of the sisters
15 of the moon…

…when I was three, my amah instructed me to eat an entire **glutinous** rice   sticky dumpling by myself. She said it would help to soften me, but I did not know what she meant until the next morning. Mama and my amah arrived by my bedside with a basin of warm water and strips of heavy white cotton. They soaked my

20 feet in the water and then proceeded to bind them with the thick wet bandages. When the bandages completed their first tight wraps around my foot, I saw red in front of my eyes and could not breathe. It felt as if my feet had shrunk into tiny insects. I began shrieking with pain; I thought I would die.

'What are you crying for?' my amah scolded me. 'Every little girl wants to
25 have her feet bound.'...

That day, my screams filled the household as long as my strength permitted. Before lunch, my father and brothers had come by to comfort me, but as the afternoon progressed only Mama and my amah appeared in the kitchen to calm me. I watched cook's **cleaver** glint up and down, heard the chicken's bones _chopping_
30 crunch beneath his blows and shrieked at the sound of it. It was as if my own _tool_
toes were breaking as they curved beneath my soles.

Bound feet take years of wrapping. The toes have to be broken slowly, carefully. Even after a girl's feet are perfectly formed, she has to keep them wrapped so they will stay in that shape. Prospective in-laws ask: 'Did she
35 complain much during her foot-binding years?' If yes, then they would think twice. She was a complainer, then, not obedient enough. Even at age three, I knew. If I was good, Mama and **Baba** would say that my feet were perfectly _Dad, Papa_
formed golden lilies, that I had been even-tempered and docile during those difficult years... If I was bad, no one would want me. I would not marry and
40 would become a disgrace to my family. And still, I cried.

For three days I sat before my amah and Mama, enduring the ritual: the removal of bloody bandages, the soaking, the rewrapping and tightening.
45 But on the fourth morning something miraculous happened. Second Brother, who could no longer bear my screams, told Mama to stop hurting me.

Pang-Mei Natasha Chang

3 ▷ Key features

The writer:
- writes about her personal experience using first-person pronouns
- addresses the reader directly and uses imperatives
- uses direct and reported speech to make the characters come alive

- How old was the writer when these events happened?
- How would she be judged in the future by her family and others?
- Who was responsible for ending her pain?

4 > Language skills

Word

A **hyphen** is a punctuation mark used to join words or parts of words together to create a new word.

❶ Find and write down the hyphenated word used in the extract for each of the following definitions. The first one has been done for you:

with stiff or straight legs = *stiff-legged*
with her hips swaying
relatives by marriage
not prone to temper tantrums
three inches in length
the process of binding the feet

❷ Make a list of hyphenated words of your own, where one of the words is *hand* or a form of the word *hand*. Here are a few to start you off:

hand-made
hand-held
single-handed

Spelling

A **suffix** is a letter or group of letters added to the end of a word to change its meaning or to create a new word.

The word *miraculous* is the adjective formed by adding the suffix *-ous* to the noun *miracle*.

Note how the spelling of the noun is affected by adding the suffix.

❶ Add the suffix *-ous* to the following nouns and note any spelling changes. Make two column headings like this. Write out the words in the noun list. Then write the adjectives which are made by adding the *-ous* suffix. The first one has been done for you.

Noun	Adjective
curiosity	*curious*
glamour	
humour	
monster	
generosity	
anxiety	
wonder	
disaster	
vigour	

Sentence

The **tense** of a verb is the form which tells us when an action happens.

Actions can happen in the past, present or future.

I walked	past tense
I walk	present tense
I will walk	future tense

The first paragraph of the extract is in the present tense.

❶ List five verbs from the first paragraph which tell us it is written in the present tense.

Here is one to start you off:

it is done

2 Where has the writer changed tense in order to write about things that happened in the past? Write your answer by completing this sentence:

> *The writer shows that she has begun to write about events in the past when she changes from the present to the past tense at....*

Imperatives are forms of verbs which command, ask or invite the reader to do something.

In the opening paragraph of the extract, the writer uses imperatives to invite the reader to imitate her actions.

> *Give me your hand...*

Find and write down two other examples of imperatives from the first paragraph.

Text

Writing can be in the **first person** (using *I, we...*), the **second person** (*you*) or the **third person** (*she, he, they, it...*).

1 Write out three sentences which describe incidents which happen to the writer where she uses the first-person pronoun. Here is one:

> *I watched cook's cleaver...*

2 Write out three sentences in the third person, where the writer writes about another person. Here is one:

> *She said it would help to soften me...*

Direct speech is a speaker's exact words reproduced in writing.

In **indirect** (or reported) **speech** we report what was said, but do not use the speaker's exact words.

In this extract the writer uses both direct and indirect reported speech to give information and to bring the characters alive.

1 Make two columns headed **Direct speech** and **Indirect** (reported) **speech**. Write each of these under the correct heading:

> *My amah said if I were good, I would grow up to be like my mother...*

> *'What are you crying for?' my amah scolded me.*

> *Prospective in-laws ask: 'Did she complain much during her foot-binding years?'*

2 Remind yourself of the rules for punctuating direct speech (page 11). Write out a short dialogue between a parent and a teenager who wants to go to an all-night party or a distant rock festival. Use direct speech.

5 ▷ Planning your own writing

Write a first-person account of a painful experience you have had. If you prefer, you can imagine the experience.

▶▶ STARTING POINTS

- Write about how it could have caused physical or emotional pain. For example:
  - an accident
  - an operation
  - a row with a friend
  - getting into trouble at home or school
  - a loss of someone you care for.

- Describe where and how it happened and your response.

- Plan how you will end your writing.

▶▶ CLUES FOR SUCCESS

- Begin by describing the context of the incident. Where did it happen? When? What had happened before?

- Address your audience directly for impact.

- Think about your feelings and sensations and share the way you felt with your reader.

- Use first-person pronouns to express personal views and feelings.

- Decide how you will describe the other people in your writing.

- Using speech is a good way to bring a character alive.

- Remember to use both direct and indirect speech.

WRITING FRAME

Use this frame to give you ideas about how you might organise your writing.

Begin by describing where the incident happened. What did you see, hear, smell?	*You can probably imagine the hospital ward...*
Introduce new characters by using speech.	*"This will sting a little," announced the young nurse cheerfully, as she rolled up my sleeve...*
What happened next?	*I could feel the sharp blade of the scalpel slice effortlessly through my flesh. At first, I felt nothing but then...*
Write about your feelings.	*Tears started to my eyes. Before I could stop, I found myself crying helplessly.*
How did it end?	*Soon, mum arrived, tears in her eyes and a frantic look on her face...*
Afterwards, what did you think?	*Two months later, the wound had healed and I was out of pain. But I will never forget...*

 REDRAFTING AND IMPROVING

- Word processors are useful for redrafting writing.
- Find and correct any spelling, punctuation or grammar errors you might have made on the first draft.
- Find opportunities to take out ordinary words and substitute stronger ones.
- Check that you have used first-person pronouns when referring to yourself.
- Have you addressed your reader directly?
- Have you included direct and indirect speech? Is direct speech correctly punctuated, with speech marks properly used?
- Make a best copy of your writing.

6 ⟩ Looking back

- **First-person pronouns** are used to write about yourself; **third-person pronouns** are used to write about other people.
- **Direct speech** brings characters alive and adds interest to writing.
- To get the attention of their readers, writers speak directly to them and use **imperative verbs** to create a feeling of authority.

Last words

1 > Purpose

In this unit you will:
- read extracts from a famous diary
- learn about style and purpose
- write an imagined diary of your own

>> Subject links: *history, geography*

2 > Diary

Captain Scott's Diary, March 1912
South Polar expedition

Friday 16 March or Saturday 17. Lost track of dates but think the last date correct. Tragedy all along the line. At lunch, the day before yesterday, poor Titus Oates said he couldn't go on; he proposed we should leave him in his sleeping bag. That we could not do, and **induced** him to come on, on the
5   afternoon march. In spite of its awful nature for him he struggled on and we made a few miles. At night he was worse and we knew the end had come.

    Should this be found I want these facts recorded. Oates's last thoughts were of his mother, but immediately before he took pride in thinking that his **regiment** would be pleased with the bold way in which he met his death. We
10   can testify to his bravery.

    He has borne intense suffering for weeks without complaint, and to the last was able and willing to discuss outside subjects. He did not – would not – give up hope to the end. He was a brave soul. This was the end. He slept through the night before last, hoping not to wake; but he woke in the morning –
15   yesterday. It was blowing a blizzard. He said, "I am just going outside and may be some time." He went out into the blizzard and we have not seen him since...

    ...We knew that poor Oates was walking to his death, but though we tried to dissuade him, we knew it was the act of a brave man and an English gentleman. We all hope to meet the end with a similar spirit, and assuredly the
20   end is not far...

   ✳ *Sunday, 18 March*. ...My right foot has gone, nearly all the toes – two days ago, I was the proud possessor of best feet. These are the steps of my downfall. Like an ass I mixed a small spoonful of curry powder with my melted **pemmican** – it gave me violent indigestion. I lay awake and in pain all night,

Margin glosses:
encouraged, coaxed

group of soldiers

dried meat

25   woke and felt done on the march; foot went and I didn't know it. A very small
measure of neglect and have a foot which is not pleasant to contemplate...
We have the last half fill of oil in our *primus* and a very small quantity of spirit
– this alone between us and thirst...

        *camping
stove, cooker*

        Monday 19 March Lunch. We camped with difficulty last night and were
30   dreadfully cold till after our supper of cold pemmican and biscuit and half a
pannikin of cocoa cooked over the spirit. Then, contrary to expectation, we
got warm and all slept well. Today we started in the usual dragging manner.
Sledge dreadfully heavy. We are 15.5 miles from the depot and ought to get
there in three days. What progress! We have two days' food but barely a day's
35   fuel. All our feet are getting bad – Wilson's best, my right foot worse, left all
right. There is no chance to nurse one's feet till we can get hot food into us.
Amputation is the least I can hope for now but will the trouble spread? That
is the serious question. The weather doesn't give us a chance – the wind from
N. to N.W. and –40 temp. today.

        cup

        *removal
of limb*

40   *Thursday 22 and 23 March*. Blizzard as bad as ever – Wilson and Bowers unable
to start – tomorrow last chance – no fuel and only one or two of food left –
must be near the end. Have decided it shall be natural – we shall march for
the depot with or without our effects and die in our tracks.

        Thursday 29 March. Since the 21st we have had a continuous gale from W.S.W.
45   and S.W. We had fuel to make two cups of tea apiece and bare food for two
days on the 20th. Every day we have been ready to start for our depot 11 miles
away, but outside the door of the tent it remains a scene of whirling drift.
I do not think we can hope for any better things now. We shall stick it out to
the end, but we are getting weaker, of course, and the end cannot be far.
50   It seems a pity, but I do not think I can write more.

                 Robert Falcon Scott

3 ▶ Key features

The writer:

- uses euphemisms to say something unpleasant in a mild way
- gives a vivid, descriptive picture of the context
- writes in a matter-of-fact style

- Who has written this diary and why?
- Where do you think it was found?
- How many different types of suffering are referred to in this extract?

4 ▶ Language skills

Word

A **euphemism** is a way of saying an unpleasant or offensive thing in a mild or pleasant way.

Writers use euphemisms to avoid expressing something ugly, harsh or hurtful.

In this extract, Scott refers to *the end* many times. He is referring to death.

❶ Write five expressions which refer to death in a euphemistic way. Here is one to start you off:

> *passed away*

❷ Here are some common euphemisms and their meanings. Match the definitions to the correct word or words and write them down. The first one has been done for you.

off colour ←	in jail
at Her Majesty's pleasure	ill
Old Nick	fat
tiddly	old
generously proportioned	drunk
of advanced years	the devil

Spelling

In the word euphemism the letters *ph* are pronounced as 'f'.

❶ List five other words which pronounce *ph* as 'f', for example *telephone*.

The sound 'f' can also be written as *gh*, for example:

> *rough*

❷ Make a list of five words which pronounce *gh* as 'f', for example *laugh*.

❸ Write a paragraph containing four words using the 'f' sound with the *gh* spelling and four words using the 'f' sound with the *ph* spelling.

Sentence

Ellipsis is where the writer chooses to leave out certain words or parts of sentences. In print this is often shown as three dots, as in line 20. (The dots indicate that some of the original diary has been left out.)

Writers also use ellipsis when writing at speed or in difficult conditions. They might not have the strength to write in full or they might be writing just for themselves, not a wider audience.

❶ Look at the entry dated *Thursday 22 and 23 March*. Work out which words are missing and write the more complete version of the entry. You could begin like this:

> *The blizzard today is as bad as it ever was. Wilson and Bowers have been unable to start on their journey.*

❷ Imagine you were writing your diary in a hurry, or in very difficult circumstances (such as on the side of a mountain!) Write an entry five sentences long. Include ellipsis to make it sound realistic. You could begin like this:

> *Weather dreadful. Wind high and cold.*

3 Which of the following reasons explain why Scott wrote in an elliptical style? You may choose more than one.

- His pen was running out
- He couldn't be bothered writing fully
- He was too exhausted to write more
- He did not expect anyone else to read what he had written
- He was cold and hungry
- He was going to rewrite it later for others to read

Suggest a reason of your own

4 Explain the reasons for your choice

Text

Writers can emphasise or stress parts of a sentence by rearranging the **order of words**. Putting words at the start of a sentence can draw attention to their importance.

He proposed we should leave him in his sleeping bag. That we could not do.

Putting *That* at the start, instead of *We could not do that*, reminds us of what we were told in the previous sentence.

1 Change the word order in these sentences from the text. The first one has been started for you.

In spite of its awful nature for him he struggled on → He struggled on in spite...

Should this be found I want these facts recorded.

We camped with difficulty last night.

Amputation is the least I can hope for now.

Every day we have been ready to start for our depot 11 miles away.

2 Pick one of your reordered sentences and write down how you think the new word order changes the meaning or emphasis.

3 Change the word order in these sentences so that different details are emphasised.

I left my home one cold frosty winter night.

Snape ripped the revolver from its holster, his eyes blazing with fury.

The kitten shivered with excitement, playing with the toy mouse.

4 Write five sentences of your own about an important moment in your life – scoring a winning goal, winning a prize, hearing some important news etc. Then write them again, changing the order of the words to find the version that you like best. You could begin like this:

My heart was pounding as I heard my name being called.

As I heard my name being called, my heart was pounding

5 ▷ Planning your own writing

Write an imagined diary of someone who endures harsh living conditions. Write four entries to cover a span of a fortnight or so.

▶▶ STARTING POINTS

You could write about:

- life on the streets – the diary of a homeless person who has been thrown out of home and has to survive by begging

- a refugee's story – survivor of war or famine who has lost family, home and been left to cope in a devastated world

- a flood victim – think about news items about recent floods and imagine how you would cope in such a situation

- living with a disability – a diary of someone who finds ordinary things a challenge. Imagine how the writer feels about life and how others react to their disability

▶▶ CLUES FOR SUCCESS

- Ask yourself what information you would want to know about the life of your subject.

- Think about your word order within sentences to make your writing dramatic.

- Use ellipsis for a natural and informal style.

- Write about the context in which you live and how it affects your life.

- Use euphemisms to soften the harshness of some expressions.

WRITING FRAME

This frame may help you get started.

Suggested contents	Example
Date 1 Establish where and when diary is written – give basic information about writer and how he/she came to be there.	I'd never have left home if I'd known it would be like this! Freezing cold pavements, damp, smelly clothes...
Date 2 Describe specific incident to give understanding of what life is like.	I was attacked by a bunch of drunken thugs last night... they thought it was fun to have a go at me...
Date 3 Describe another day. Give details of everyday life.	My clothes stink and so do I! My stomach aches from hunger so much that I ...
Date 4 Shape some thoughts about your life.	It's hard to have any hope...

REDRAFTING AND IMPROVING

- Have you written in a way that is appropriate, using ellipsis for realism?
- Is your diary convincing, using realistic details about your environment?
- Have you ordered your words in the best way to make events sound as dramatic as possible?

6 Looking back

- **Ellipsis** can be used when you are writing quickly, or under difficult circumstances, or when you are creating these effects
- You can achieve different effects by changing the **word order** of your sentences. Changing the order helps to stress certain words.
- **Euphemisms** can be used to avoid using unpleasant or harsh words.

Final moments

In this unit you will:
- read an extract from an autobiography
- learn how the writer shares a sense of excitement
- write an autobiographical extract of your own

▶▶ **Subject links:** *sport, media*

2 ▶ **Autobiography**

Managing My Life

The Bayern colours had already been tied on to the Cup in readiness for the presentation to the winners and Lennart Johansson, president of UEFA, was making his way under the stands to perform the ceremony. Then, as the world knows, something almost miraculous occurred. Put starkly, what happened was that two David Beckham corners led to two goals by Teddy Sheringham and Ole Gunnar Solksjaer but, as somebody suggested to me, such a description is about as adequate as saying that the Battle of Hastings was settled on a cut-eye decision. The magical transformation

crowded into less than two minutes of stoppage time at the Nou Camp deserves more expansive treatment, and I will try to provide it when the Barcelona experience takes its natural place in the story I am setting out to tell. Surely nowhere in football's past was there ever such an improbable or electrifying finish to one of the great occasions of the game. Bayern, who were totally gone after Teddy Sheringham scored and couldn't have hoped to live with us if the match had carried into extra time, were like corpses when the amazing speed of Solskjaer's reactions enabled him to jut out a leg and turn the ball forcefully into the roof of their net. We were like dervishes, and so were our supporters. The European Cup was coming to Old Trafford for the second time, after a gap of thirty-one years, and on what would have been Sir Matt Busby's 90th birthday. For me, the result meant arriving at a peak of aspiration that had sometimes seemed unreachable. In the turmoil of celebration, there was a private corner of my mind that was recalling some of the key stages of the climb. I remembered... but perhaps I had better begin at the beginning.

Alex Ferguson

3 ▷ Key features

The writer:
- writes in the first person
- uses parenthesis to add detail
- uses specialist vocabulary

- Where did these events take place?
- What was unique about the occasion?
- How long had Manchester United had to wait to win the trophy for a second time?

4 > Language skills

Word

A **noun** is a word that names a person, place, object or idea.

Nouns can be divided into four types.

Common nouns are the names of objects:

> man, ball

Proper nouns are names of individual people, places, organisations or titles. A proper noun begins with a capital letter:

> David Beckham, Manchester United

Collective nouns are names of groups of people or things:

> team, herd

Abstract nouns are names of feelings, qualities or ideas:

> happiness, skill, hatred

1 Look at this list of nouns from the extract and pick out the proper nouns. Write the proper nouns down, giving them capital letters.

> winners   bayern   football
> lennart   johansson   stands
> teddy   sheringham
> goals   battle of hastings
> barcelona   story   match
> corpses   sir matt busby
> european cup   supporters
> celebration   aspiration
> speed   old trafford

2 Make three columns and give each column the title of one kind of noun (common, proper and abstract). Write the above nouns in the right columns.

3 Why has the word *Cup* been written with a capital letter in the extract?

Spelling

A **syllable** is a single section of a word when it is spoken out loud. For example, the word *presentation* has four syllables:

> pre-sent-a-tion

Breaking up a word into its syllables helps to make long words easier to spell and pronounce.

1 Here is a list of words from the extract, each containing several syllables. Write the words in a list and then write the word again, showing how it breaks down into syllables. The first one has been done for you.

> president   **pre – sid – ent**
> miraculous
> description
> transformation
> expansive
> experience
> electrifying
> celebration

(There will be more than one way in which to break up some of these words into syllables.)

Sentence

If we add a word or phrase to a sentence, using commas, dashes or brackets, we say that the word or phrase is in **parenthesis**. (To pronounce it, put the stress on the *ren*.)

> *Then, as the world knows, something almost miraculous occurred.*

1 Write down the sentence above, underlining the part in parenthesis.

2 Write the sentence again without the parenthesis.

3 Write down why you think the writer put in the additional information.

Was it:

- to make his statement more forceful?
- to give more information?
- to help the reader to understand that he is writing about something important?
- to make it sound as if he is speaking to the reader?

4 Find and write down three more examples of parenthesis from the extract. In each case, explain in writing why the writer added the word or phrase to his sentence.

Text

The words and phrases used by particular groups of people who share the same job or interest are called **specialist vocabulary**. Specialist vocabulary is sometimes called **jargon**.

In this extract, the writer uses specialist terms related to football. He relies on the fact that his readers will know something about the game.

1 Explain what the following words and phrases mean. The first has been done for you.

The Bayern colours	Ribbons in the colours of the winning team which are tied to the handles of the trophy
two David Beckham corners	
stoppage time	
extra time	
turn the ball	
the roof of their net	
the Barcelona experience	

2 Write a list of other words and phrases of your own which relate to football, or any other sport.

5 ▷ Planning your own writing

Write an exciting opening to your own autobiography.

▶▶ STARTING POINTS

- Think about thrilling or important moments from your own life – victories, accidents, holidays, first time doing something, mastering a new skill, meeting a special friend.

- Select one event which will be especially interesting to the reader.

- Reflect on the details of the occasion that stand out in your mind – weather, location, people, sounds.

- Remember how you felt and how other people around reacted. Have your feelings changed over time?

- Write down some words and phrases which will create a sense of the context in which the incident happened.

▶▶ CLUES FOR SUCCESS

- Write your opening sentence carefully to grab the attention of your reader.

- Use the personal pronoun *I*.

- Describe in detail what was happening, using parenthesis to give your writing additional detail.

- Describe the context, using words and phrases which make the readers feel as if they are there.

- Don't finish your story – leave the reader wanting more.

▶▶ REDRAFTING AND IMPROVING

- Have you used the first-person pronoun *I* when referring to yourself?

- Have you included the kind of detail that makes the reader interested in your writing?

- Have you used parenthesis when including additional information?

- Have you described the context in which the incident happened, using appropriate vocabulary?

- Have you written about your feelings?

- Have you left your reader wanting to read on, by creating suspense?

WRITING FRAMES

Use one of these writing frames to give you ideas.

Writing frame A

For years I had wanted to _____

_____

Suddenly, I was _____

The atmosphere was _____

Around me _____

I could hear, faintly, the sound of _____

I felt as if _____

I remembered back to _____

I should explain how it all started _____

Writing frame B

It was the most memorable, amazing moment of my life, a time I would never forget.

I was _____

Then _____

Never have I felt so _____

What happened was _____

But the story does not end there! _____

6 ▷ Looking back

- Writers use **parenthesis** to insert additional information into the sentence.

- Writing often includes **specialist vocabulary** if it is aimed at a particular audience.

On the verge of greatness

1 ▷ **Purpose**

In this unit you will:
- read an article about a famous athlete
- see how the writer describes his subject
- write your own article about someone

▷▷ **Subject links:** *physical education, religious education*

2 ▷ **Sports journalism**

El Guerrouj on the verge of greatness

El Guerrouj

The Red Shadow floats over the track like the desert wind wafting across the surface of the sand; so tenderly do his spikes touch the ground, they say Hicham El Guerrouj does not leave 5 footprints behind him in the dust on his training runs through the Atlas Mountains in northern Africa.

Holder of the 1,500 metres and one-mile world records, the slight figure in the 10 scarlet vest and shorts of Morocco inspires a sense of wonderment even among those who reigned before him. 'Seb Coe was a beautiful sight,' said Australian icon Herb Elliot as El Guerrouj lapped the Olympic 15 track in an effortless blur, 'but this young man is something else. He makes a gazelle look like a duck-billed platypus. Barring accidents, we could hold the medal ceremony right now.' 20

Barring accidents. When the men's 1,500m first round heats are staged on Monday, El Guerrouj will offer up a prayer Elliot's words are not prophetic, for in the final in Atlanta four years ago, 25 at the instant he pulled out to overtake Noureddine Morceli at the bell sounding the last lap, his knee caught the Algerian's heel and he crashed to the ground, ultimately finishing 12th and last. 30

'I carry an old newspaper everywhere I go which shows me weeping after I crossed the line,' El Guerrouj said through a French interpreter. 'I have brought it with me to Sydney to remind 35 me that the fates often have a will of their own.'

'I knew my destiny was to run for Morocco'

Only 21 at the time, El Guerrouj was still sobbing in the stadium tunnel when he was handed a mobile phone by his coach. 40 '"Your king wishes to speak to you," he told me.' Down the line came the gentle voice of King Hassan. 'For the Moroccan people you are the true Olympic champion,' he said. 'Forget about this day 45 and begin preparing for your own coronation in Sydney.'

'When I came off the track in Atlanta I felt I had let down 30 million of my people,' El Guerrouj said. 'I wanted to 50 go into the hills and hide myself away. I believed I would never race again. The King's words were like the sun coming out again after a terrible storm. From that moment I knew my destiny was to 55 run for Morocco.'

A millionaire whose Islamic faith demands that he scorns the familiar trappings of wealth, El Guerrouj returns home to his family's modest restaurant in 60 the orange-growing region of the country at periodic intervals to prepare and serve free meals for the poor.

'In Islam, we are taught to believe that no-one, no matter how rich, famous or 65 successful, is better than anyone else. I have been given a gift and I must use that to bring happiness and pride to those who may be materially less fortunate than myself. 70

It is the thoughts a man keeps in his heart which are important, not the amount of money he keeps in a chest under his bed.'

El Guerrouj's most prized possession 75 is a framed document signed by all 216 living former one-mile world record holders from Sydney Wooderson to Roger Bannister to Seb Coe to Morceli. His own signature and time of 3.43.13 80 appears at the bottom in preparation to be handed over to his successor. 'It will never happen,' he grinned boyishly. 'I want to set a time that will never be beaten in my lifetime.' 85

Robert Philip

3 ▸ Key features

In this text the writer:

- begins with a dramatic simile to create a vivid image
- uses alliteration to create patterns of sound
- includes quotations from several sources

- How did El Guerrouj lose the final at Atlanta?
- What made him recover from his disappointment?
- What do the four men mentioned in the last paragraph have in common?

4 ⟩ Language skills

Word

The **apostrophe** (') is a punctuation mark with two different uses:

1 to show that a letter or group letters has been missed out (omission)

2 to show possession or ownership:

> *the Algerian's heel — the King's words — El Guerrouj's most prized possession — his family's modest restaurant — all the champions' medals — the medal winners' podium*

1 Rewrite the following, using the apostrophe to show possession. The first one has been done for you:

> *the lamp of the miner → miner's lamp*
> *the lesson of the teacher*
> *the trophy of the winner*
> *the skateboard of John*
> *the report of the pupil*
> *the bags of the girls*
> *the school of the boys*

Spelling

Silent letters are letters which are not sounded when the word is spoken.

Two common examples are the *b* in *comb* and the *l* in *calm*.

1 Find and write down three words in the article on El Guerrouj (to line 40) which contain silent letters.

2 The silent letter *k* is often found at the beginning of words and is often followed by *n*. Make a list of ten words containing a silent *k*. Here are three to start your list:

> *knit, knowledge, knot*

3 The silent *g* is often followed by *n*. Here is a list of words which contain a silent *g*:

> *gnaw   sovereign   sign   foreign,*
> *gnat   gnome   assignment   gnash*

Match the following definitions to the words above which contain a silent *g* and write them down. The first one has been done for you.

chew   *gnaw*
coming from another
    country
monarch or ruler
small irritating insect
ugly garden statue
a task or job
to write one's name
to clash the teeth

Sentence

Alliteration is the repetition of initial consonant sounds to create an effect.

The snake slithered and slid through the grass.

❶ Write a paragraph of your own using at least five examples of alliteration. Write about either a terrible storm or an animal of your choice.

A **simile** is a way of comparing things in an unusual or unexpected way, so that the writer creates an **image** in the reader's mind. A simile uses the words *like* or *as*.

The Red Shadow floats over the track like the desert wind wafting across the surface of the sand.

❷ Write your answers to the following questions about this introductory sentence.

- Why does El Guerrouj have the nickname *The Red Shadow*?
- If something *floats*, how does it move?
- What does the word *wafting* suggest about the desert wind?
- Find the simile which describes the way El Guerrouj felt about the King of Morocco's words.

❸ Write a sentence of your own, using a simile, which describes the face of a triumphant athlete crossing the finishing line. You might begin like this:

As she crossed the line, the smile on Cathy Freeman's face was like...

Text

Quotation marks are used to mark the beginning and end of someone's actual words when they are quoted in a piece of writing. They can either be single (' ') or double (" "). When they are used to show that a word or phrase is being quoted from someone else, they are known as quotation marks.

❶ Draw up a table listing the speakers who have been quoted in the article, their roles, the main content of what they say and why they are quoted. If a person has been quoted more than once, list each occasion separately. The first has been done for you.

speaker	Herb Elliot
role	Australian runner
content	comments on El Guerrouj's qualities as a runner
why quoted	to show El Guerrouj's reputation among runners

5 ▶ Planning your own writing

Write an article about a person you admire. It may be a famous person or someone you know personally. In your writing, try to bring out your subject's special qualities and achievements. Include the opinions of other people.

▶▶ STARTING POINTS

Your article could be about:

- a sportsman or star of music, film or media

- someone who has overcome problems to succeed in their chosen field

- someone who has set a good example to others

- an adult who has inspired you or helped you

- someone whose work has helped others, either on a large or on a small scale

▶▶ CLUES FOR SUCCESS

- Begin with a strong and vivid image which describes the subject in a dramatic way, either at work or engaged in some activity.

- Use quotations from other people to show the subject's reputation.

- Use quotations from the subject to give an insight into his or her beliefs and feelings.

- Think about the words you choose and use alliteration to create patterns of sound in order to make your language memorable and interesting.

▶▶ REDRAFTING AND IMPROVING

- Have you succeeded in giving a true picture of your subject?

- Did you use a dramatic image to create interest in your subject at the start?

- Have you used alliteration for sound patterns?

- Have you given opinions about your subject using quotations from other sources?

- Have you given an insight into your subject's background and beliefs, as well as describing his or her achievements?

WRITING FRAME

Use this writing frame to give you ideas about how to proceed.

Describe your subject using a strong, vivid image.	*When X walks into the room, there is a sudden hush as if...*
Quote a friend or colleague to pay tribute to the subject.	*'X has the most extraordinary effect on people,' confided...*
Write about the subject's background and/or beliefs.	*X comes from an ordinary, rather humble background, but there was a strong sense of spiritual values...*
Write about the subject's achievements.	*In the past ten years, X has achieved...*
Finish with a quote from the subject	*'I believe...*

6 ▷ Looking back

- Writers use **imagery**, including **similes**, to create strong and vivid pictures in the reader's mind. These images are often used at the start of a piece of writing to generate interest in the subject.

- **Alliteration** is used to create patterns of sound and to make language memorable.

- Newspaper articles use **quotation** from various sources, including the subject of the article, to give a range of opinions.

I don't like to be beside the seaside!

1 > **Purpose**

In this unit you will:

- read a piece of travel writing which is written from a personal viewpoint
- think about the relationship between a writer and the reader
- write a passage in which you express your own beliefs and bias

Subject links: *mathematics, geography*

2 > Travel writing

Blackpool

"Greetings from Blackpool"

Blackpool – *and I don't care how many times you hear this, it never stops being amazing* – *attracts more visitors every year than Greece and has more holiday beds than the whole of Portugal. It consumes more chips per capita than anywhere else on the planet. (It gets through 40 acres of potatoes a day.) It has the largest concentration of rollercoasters in Europe. It has the continent's second most popular tourist attraction, the 42 acre Pleasure Beach, whose 6.5 million annual visitors*

are exceeded in number only by those going to the Vatican. It has the most famous illuminations. And on Friday and Saturday nights it has more public toilets than anywhere else in Britain; elsewhere they call them doorways.

Whatever you may think of the place, it does what it does very well – or if not very well at least very successfully. In the past twenty years, during a period in which the number of Britons taking traditional seaside holidays has declined by a fifth, Blackpool has increased its visitor numbers by 7 per cent and built tourism into a £250-million-a-year industry – no small achievement when you consider the British climate, the fact that Blackpool is ugly, dirty and a long way from anywhere, that its sea is an open toilet, and its attractions nearly all cheap, provincial and dire.

Bill Bryson

3 ⟩ Key features

The writer:
- uses statistics to emphasise the popularity of Blackpool
- includes humour to get his message across
- expresses a personal viewpoint which is different to that of many people

≫ ● Which key facts show that Blackpool is a very popular resort?
● How does Bill Bryson describe Blackpool, in his opinion?
● Which two things mentioned make Blackpool attractive to visitors?

4 Language skills

Word

A **preposition** is a word such as *on*, *under*, *by* or *for*. It is usually followed by a **noun phrase**:

*Blackpool is **on** the coast.*

Per is a preposition meaning *through*, *by* or *by means of*; it is frequently found with other Latin words to make phrases used in statistical and financial information:

***per** capita,* ***per** cent,* ***per** annum*

1 Write five sentences using *per* in different ways. For example:

*My eye blinks three times **per** second.*

2 Make a list of the kind of books and documents in which you might find *per* written. Try to think of at least ten examples from different areas, such as a geography textbook or medical records.

Spelling

An *-ier* **suffix** can be added to the end of a word to intensify its meaning:

ugly – uglier, lively – livelier (note that the words have dropped the *y* endings to add the *-ier*)

These words are used when you want to compare one thing against another:

*Mudsea is **dirtier** than any other seaside town.*

*People are **happier** when they are in Blackpool.*

(This is called the comparative form of the adjective.)

1 Write six words that have this *-ier* ending which could be used to describe Blackpool. Choose three that could make it sound nicer than other places and three that make it sound unpleasant if you compare it to another town.

2 Write six sentences using each one of your words.

Sentence

Writers sometimes use **long sentences** when they have a large number of facts to get across. Bill Bryson has written a very long sentence in the second paragraph. It starts with *In the past twenty years...*

1 Identify all the different pieces of information that form part of the sentence.

Write smaller, simpler sentences for each part but do not change the meaning.

You may have to add words or change the order of what is written.

Here is an example of what you have to do using the first sentence from the extract.

Blackpool attracts more visitors than Greece.

Blackpool has more holiday beds than the whole of Portugal.

No matter how many times you hear this it never stops being amazing.

2 Read Bill Bryson's sentence and your sentences aloud to yourself. You will find that they sound very different.

Write the answers to these questions:

- What is different about the sound of these two ways of writing sentences?
- Which style do you prefer and why?
- Why do you think Bill Bryson chose to use these kinds of sentences?

Text

Bill Bryson is a very successful travel writer. His books are popular because of his style of writing; he doesn't just describe the countries he goes to but he gives his own very personal viewpoint about the places. He is good at remembering that he is writing for an audience: he creates a **relationship with the reader**.

In this short passage he does this in three ways:

- He addresses the reader directly.
- He uses humour to make the reader laugh.
- He includes fascinating facts to keep the reader interested.

1 Find and write down an example of each one of these from the extract.

2 Write two or three sentences to explain how Bryson has succeeded in creating a good reader/writer relationship and give the reasons for your opinion.

Many writers use statistics (facts and figures) to support their accounts.

3 Write down three examples of Bryson's use of statistics. Next to each one, write a sentence to explain how the statistic adds interest to the description of Blackpool.

59

5 ▷ Planning your own writing

Write a short passage in which you express your strong dislike of something that is popular with many other people.

⟫ STARTING POINTS

You could base your writing on one of the ideas below:

- another popular holiday destination or visitor attraction
- a television programme that is the favourite of many viewers
- a very successful pop star or group
- a film that everyone thinks is great
- an extremely popular fast food chain

⟫ REDRAFTING AND IMPROVING

- Read your piece of writing out loud. Does it sound right?
- Have you used some comparative words with *-ier* endings?
- Do your sentences sound like you are speaking to your reader?
- Have you given your reader some surprises?
- Do you really get your own viewpoint across?

⟫ CLUES FOR SUCCESS

- Build a relationship between yourself and your reader.
- Provide a contrast between your view and that of most other people.
- Include information that might surprise or interest the reader.
- Use humour if possible.
- Try to create a distinctive style of your own.
- Avoid being nasty, as readers might dislike you rather than the topic of your passage.

WRITING FRAMES

Use one of these writing frames to help you get started.

Writing frame A

I know most people think...

It never ceases to amaze me that...

Wherever I go I hear everyone saying...

The most surprising thing to me is...

Writing frame B

Plan carefully.

Choose your subject well and list all the evidence you have of its popularity.

Think of some funny ideas you could use.

Make use of facts and figures if you can.

Make a list of all the words you can to describe how you feel about your topic.

Experiment with different kinds of sentence structures to make it sound like you are talking to your readers.

6 Looking back

- **Per** is a useful preposition when working with numbers.
- **Long sentences** can make writing sound more interesting.
- A writer's style can create a **relationship with the reader**.
- Writers can use **statistics** to inform the reader and also to capture their interest.

Tyranny and revenge at sea

In this unit you will:
- read two historical accounts
- learn about chronology in information
- write a chronological account

» **Subject links:** *geography, history*

2 **Historical accounts**

Mutiny on the *Bounty*

H.M.S. *Bounty* left Spithead on 23rd December, 1787, to carry a cargo of bread-fruit plants from Tahiti, in the South Pacific, to the British colonies in the West Indies. Captain Cook
5 had discovered the fruit and the Navy Board had decided to grow it in the West Indies as food for the slaves on the plantations. The *Bounty* was a small ship of 215 tons and the 46 men aboard were very cramped. The captain, Lieutenant William Bligh, was a good
10 sailor, but he had a terrible temper and behaved like a tyrant. The voyage out was long and hard – the *Bounty* did not reach Tahiti until 26th October, 1788. On the way there were fierce storms and, when rations became short, Bligh made the crew eat bad fruit.
15 The *Bounty* stayed nearly six months at Tahiti and the crew became idle in the tropical heat. When the ship sailed again on 4th April, 1789, Bligh found that the crew was unwilling to take orders. Bligh had a particular dislike for Fletcher Christian, the second-in-

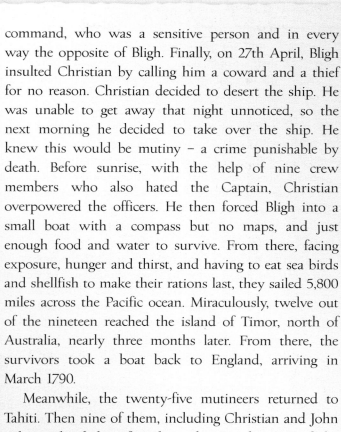

command, who was a sensitive person and in every 20
way the opposite of Bligh. Finally, on 27th April, Bligh
insulted Christian by calling him a coward and a thief
for no reason. Christian decided to desert the ship. He
was unable to get away that night unnoticed, so the
next morning he decided to take over the ship. He 25
knew this would be mutiny – a crime punishable by
death. Before sunrise, with the help of nine crew
members who also hated the Captain, Christian
overpowered the officers. He then forced Bligh into a
small boat with a compass but no maps, and just 30
enough food and water to survive. From there, facing
exposure, hunger and thirst, and having to eat sea birds
and shellfish to make their rations last, they sailed 5,800
miles across the Pacific ocean. Miraculously, twelve out
of the nineteen reached the island of Timor, north of 35
Australia, nearly three months later. From there, the
survivors took a boat back to England, arriving in
March 1790.

Meanwhile, the twenty-five mutineers returned to
Tahiti. Then nine of them, including Christian and John 40
Adams, decided to found a colony with some of the
native Polynesians on the remote Pitcairn Islands, where
they would be unlikely to be found. The other sixteen
stayed at Tahiti. In 1791 H.M.S. *Pandora* arrived in search
of them. They were captured and sent back to England 45
for trial, and three of them were executed. The Pitcairn
colonists were not discovered until an American ship
accidentally landed there in 1808. John Adam was the
only mutineer still alive and he said Christian had been
murdered many years before. No-one knows the truth, 50
as one of the crew claimed he had secretly made his
way back to England quite soon after the mutiny and
had even been seen in the streets of Devonport.

Prudence Mumford

Four men in a boat

On July 5th, 1884, three men and a cabin boy were shipwrecked from their small boat and cast adrift in a 14 ft. dinghy. They were well out in the Atlantic and 300 miles from the nearest trade route. They had no water and their sole provisions were two tins of vegetables. They tried
5 unsuccessfully to catch fish, but by killing a turtle and catching rain water in their capes, they managed to survive for sixteen days.

The captain, who had shown great character and practical ability in keeping the others alive, had improvised a sail from their clothing and calculated with the aid of a compass that within one week they would have reached the South
10 American trade route. But already their food and water supplies were exhausted and there seemed no hope of surviving that long.

The cabin boy, who had disobeyed the captain's orders by drinking sea-water, was now in a coma and not expected to live longer than three days.

All other efforts of survival having failed, the captain now decided that one
15 man should die in order that three should live. In view of his condition, and also because he had no children and no mother, the cabin boy seemed the obvious but unfortunate victim. This was eventually decided upon although one of the other men, Edmund Brooks, refused to be party to the killing.

Accordingly, the boy's throat was slit, his blood drunk before it could
20 congeal and his liver eaten while it was still warm. All three men, including Brooks, fed on the body.

Five days later, on July 29th, having drifted 1,050 miles in 24 days, they were picked up by a German ship which landed them in Falmouth on September 6th. Having made no attempt to conceal what they had done, the captain
25 immediately made a full statement to the authorities. All three regretted their action but felt that, in the circumstances, they were quite justified in the action they took. Two days later, they were charged with murder on the high seas.

Because of the many implications of the case, which was by now arousing considerable public interest, the hearing was transferred from the local Assizes
30 at Exeter to the High Court in London, where it was heard before Lord Chief Justice Coleridge on December 4th, 1884.

R W Taylor

3 ▷ Key features

The writers:
- use factual detail and give specific dates and details
- include complex and compound sentences
- organise the information chronologically, listing the important events

- How do you know these accounts are fact?
- How long had each group of men been cast away at sea?
- For each text, explain who was charged with what crimes.

4 Language skills

Word

An **abstract noun** is the label given to something we cannot see, hear or touch, often an emotion, feeling or idea.

Examples include nouns such as *anger*, *jealousy* or *happiness*. Words like *freedom* or *slavery* or *loneliness* are also abstract nouns.

1 Write down the two abstract nouns used in the title of this unit and give their meanings.

2 Write a sentence to explain why having these two words in the title might make you want to read the two accounts that follow.

3 Find and write down the abstract nouns used in the first account. Use the clues to help you.

e__o__r_   h__g__   th__t
t__th   d_s_i_e _u__y

4 Make abstract nouns from these adjectives used in the first account. The first one has been done for you.

Adjective	Abstract noun
hard	hardness
idle	
sensitive	
long	
fierce	

5 Look at the second account and find the two abstract nouns which label the captain's qualities.

6 Write your own two sentences, each containing one of the abstract nouns you have just found.

Spelling

Ranks in the armed forces often have names which are difficult to spell.

1 Learn this list:

captain	*lieutenant*
admiral	*midshipman*
corporal	*sergeant*
brigadier	*colonel*

A mnemonic is a way of helping you to remember something.

In the word *captain*, the difficult part of the spelling is the letter group *ain*. You might remember this by remembering *the cap**tain** is a p**ain** in the neck*.

In the word *colonel*, the difficulty is in the first four letters which do not spell like they sound. You might remember these by making up a silly sentence where the words correspond to the letters of the word:

choice of lamb or nice, early lettuce

2 Make up and write mnemonics of your own to help you to remember the spellings of the list of ranks.

4 > Language skills

Sentence

A **comma** is a punctuation mark used to break up sentences and make them easier to understand.

In these texts, commas are used:

- **to make a list**

    ... facing exposure, hunger and thirst...

- **in pairs, to include additional information (this is called parenthesis)**

    The cabin boy, who had already disobeyed the captain's orders by drinking sea-water, was now in a coma...

- **to separate the main clauses of a long sentence**

    He was unable to get away that night unnoticed, so the next morning he decided to take over the ship.

- **to mark adverbial phrases near the starts of sentences:**

    Before sunrise,
    Five days later,

❶ Find and write out another example from the texts of the use of commas:

- for a list
- for parenthesis
- to separate clauses in a longer sentence and
- to mark adverbial phrases

❷ Write out these sentences and underline the main clause in each:

I decided to wear my old boots as the snow was now falling hard.

After we had eaten enough to keep us going, we set out on the last lap.

While Charlie was moaning, we crept out of the room.

They won't win if they carry on playing like this.

We can't get there unless someone gives us a lift.

Text

Chronology is the arrangement of events in the order in which they happen.

In these accounts the writers describe events in chronological order.

❶ Using the information given in either account, draw a time-line to show the events in the order in which they occurred. Here is the start for each account.

Account 1
23 December 1787
Bounty *leaves Spithead bound for Tahiti*

Account 2
5 July 1884
Four men are shipwrecked

A **sentence** is a group of words which makes sense on its own.

Sentences can be divided into three main types: simple, compound and complex. Writers use all three sentence types in their writing.

A **simple sentence** consists of one clause. It says just one thing and contains only one main verb.

> *H.M.S.* Bounty *left Spithead on 23rd December, 1787.*

A **compound sentence** is when we join two or more simple sentences together with *or, and* or *but*.

> *They had no water and their sole provisions were two tins of vegetables*

A **complex sentence** is when we use a different conjunction (such as *because* or *when*) to show how two or more clauses are joined together in meaning. The conjunction often goes at the beginning of the sentence.

> ***When*** *the ship sailed again on 4th April, 1789, Bligh found that the crew was unwilling to take orders.*

1 From each text find and write out another example of a) a simple sentence b) a compound sentence and c) a complex sentence.

2 Combine these simple sentences together by using conjunctions to make compound sentences. Write them out.

> *I am going out to see a film. I shall be back at ten o'clock.*

> *City and United both played well. The match ended in a draw.*

> *I was very late. I ran all the way there.*

3 Combine these sentences to make complex sentences. Write them out, underlining the main clause in the sentence.

> *The house is large. We can just afford the rent.*

> *The fox kept attacking the chickens. We built a new fence.*

> *She wrote the letter. I watched from the door.*

The **structure** of a text is the way it is put together in paragraphs.

In these accounts, **paragraphs** are used to organise the sequence of information.

1 Write a simple sentence to sum up what each paragraph is about. The first one has been done for you.

> 1 *Four men are shipwrecked.*

2 Write down the dates or other clues which writers use to tell us the time between events.

5 ▷ Planning your own writing

Write an account of a true event. It might be something from your own experience or something you have learned about or been taught. Organise your information clearly so your reader can understand what happened.

▷▷ STARTING POINTS

You account could be about:

- a battle, a siege, a famous rescue or feat of bravery

- the birth of a new child in your family

- a gladiator fight in a Roman arena

- an incident in the life of a person you admire

- a wedding or family celebration

▷▷ CLUES FOR SUCCESS

- Plan the key events in your account.

- Decide how many paragraphs you will use. You could use a three-paragraph model (background, incident, result) or you could use a new paragraph for each key event.

- Make sure you include information about dates and times.

- Use correct names and accurate spelling.

- Use a combination of sentence types to vary your writing style and to give a lot of information.

- Use the comma to help you to punctuate sentences.

▷▷ REDRAFTING AND IMPROVING

- Have you written in paragraphs, carefully organising the information in the order in which things happened?

- Have you written in a variety of sentence types? Are your sentences punctuated properly, with capital letters and full stops? Have you used appropriate connectives to link ideas or information together?

- Have you used the comma to help you to punctuate your longer sentences?

>> WRITING FRAMES

Use one of these writing frames as a model to help you get started.

Writing frame A

My account begins on (date) in (place)...

Suddenly, things began to happen!

After it was all over...

Writing frame B

Saturday 23 July was the first day of...

Three days later...

After an hour or so...

The following week...

By the middle of August...

Months later...

6 > Looking back

- In an account, **chronology** is important to help the reader to understand the order of events.

- Use **paragraphs** to show the order of events and to **structure** your information.

- Using a **variety of sentence types** adds variety to your writing and allows you to include extra detail in longer sentences.

- You can punctuate longer sentences by using a **comma**.

Wonderful Wales

1 **Purpose**

In this unit you will:
- read extracts from a travel feature and an encyclopaedia
- learn about matching style to audience and purpose
- write about a place in two different styles

» **Subject links:** *geography, history, media, travel and tourism*

2 **Travel feature**

Anglesey diary

5.30 p.m.

We drive through Beaumaris, stopping briefly for a glimpse at the magnificent stone castle built by the English monarch Edward I which rang the death-knell for the mighty kingdom of Gwynedd. We head south-west towards Newborough, a place name that sticks out like a sore thumb among the surrounding Welsh villages. To make room for his new castle and town at Beaumaris (another foreign-sounding name derived from the French, beaumarais, meaning 'fair marsh'), Edward drove out the local people and resettled them in a new borough specifically created for them – hence the name. Little can be seen of Edward's borough but one treasure from an earlier period still remains. At the height of Gwynedd's power, in the so-called 'Age of the Princes', the royal palace of Rhosyr was built close to what later became Newborough. Excavations are underway right now, and anyone interested in Celtic history will be fascinated by the skeleton of this 13th century 'llys' or palace which lay buried in the sand for hundreds of years.

7.00 p.m.

We're starting to flag now, so what better than an early evening stroll through the local pine woods and onto Newborough Sands to watch the sun set? It's a magical place that gives off an aura of peace and tranquillity. It's hard to believe that a thousand years ago it was at the very heart of the most powerful kingdom in Wales.

8.00 p.m.

A brief stop for a shower and a change of clothes, then back to Beaumaris for dinner at the Olde Bull's Head. Downstairs is a typical half-timbered pub lounge complete with log fire, comfy old sofas and lots of brass and copper hanging on the walls. But when we're ushered upstairs for our meal our minds are well and truly blown. I thought we'd be eating in Ye Olde Dining Halle, but find myself in what looks like a brand new swanky Kensington restaurant.

The décor is purple and white, there's sea-grass matting on the floor and elegant minimalist tables and chairs. As for food... I won't dwell on the mouth-watering tartare of marinated sea-bass or the sea trout on a bed of black spaghetti with freshwater prawns. But allow me to wax lyrical about my side salad. My impression is that the job of preparing the salad is usually given to some bored lad on work experience, who serves up something limp, lacklustre and totally devoid of imagination. But this was the side salad of the gods. Its contents included quail's eggs, artichokes, avocado, wild mushrooms and the sexiest black olives it's ever been my privilege to swallow. Top nosh!

12 midnight

Where shall we go tomorrow — Parys Mountain, the National Trust house and gardens of Plas Newydd, Cors Goch Nature Reserve, the Holyhead Breakwater Country Park? Wherever we decide to go, one thing's absolutely clear. Anglesey is a very special place.

Tony Robinson

Encyclopaedia entry

ANGLESEY *(North Wales)*, island and county, is separated from the mainland by the Menai straits. It has an area of 276 square miles and is mainly lowland. Many kinds of sea birds are found on the rocky coast and on the little islands of Puffin and Llanddwyn. Beaumaris is the county town. The climate is drier than the rest of Wales. Holyhead has a regular passenger service to Ireland. The tubular railway bridge over the Menai straits was built by Robert Stevenson and the road bridge beside it by Thomas Telford.

Anglesey was a stronghold of the Welsh druids until the time of its capture by the Romans in AD 61. Later it held out against the attacks by the English; Edward I however succeeded in conquering the island and reinforced his position by building a fortress at Beaumaris.

3 > Key features

The writers:
- have clear purposes in writing their texts
- compose their writing to suit their audience
- use fact and opinion where appropriate

- Why was the building of Beaumaris Castle important in the history of Anglesey?
- Which of the two texts goes furthest back into the history of the island?
- How is Anglesey connected to the mainland?

4 Language skills

Word

The explanation of a word's origin is called its **etymology**. Many of the words and place names in Tony Robinson's article are not originally from English at all, but from French or Welsh.

1 Look at this list of words from the texts. Work with a partner to say them aloud as accurately as you can.

Beaumaris	Menai
décor	Gwynedd
Cors Goch	llys
restaurant	Parys Mountain
Plas Newydd	Llanddwyn
tartare	Rhosyr

2 Separate the words into two lists, labelled *French* and *Welsh*. For each word, underline the group of letters which look like French or Welsh spellings.

Spelling

A number of English words include the *eau* pattern. Most of them are originally from French.

1 The word 'Beaumaris' comes from the French language. What other common English word also begins with the French 'beau' which means 'fair' or 'lovely'?

Sentence

A **rhetorical question** does not require an answer but is used to achieve an effect.

For example, someone might say: 'Why should I care?'

1 Find and write down two rhetorical questions used by Tony Robinson.

2 Why does he use these questions? Here is a list of possible answers. Write down which you think are the most likely. You may select as many as you like.

- He really does not know the answer.
- He wants to sound informal and friendly.
- He wants to stress how much there is to do on the island.
- He wants to stress that the island is a wonderful place.
- He wants the reader to get involved with the text by thinking about answers.
- He wants to show that Anglesey has something for everyone.
- He wants to show how much he has enjoyed his visit.

3 There are no rhetorical questions in the encyclopaedia entry. Why do you think this is so?

Tense is the form of the verb which shows when something happens – either the present, the past or the future.

4 Tony Robinson mainly uses the present tense in his writing. Explain in writing why you think he uses this tense.

5 Find and write down five examples of verbs in the present tense from the diary.

6 Find the place where he switches to the future tense. Explain why this happens at this point in the text.

7 The encyclopaedia entry is written using a mixture of past and present tense. Draw two columns and label them **Past tense** and **Present tense**. Go through the encyclopaedia entry and pick out the verbs or verb phrases. Write each of them in the correct column.

8 Look at the verbs in the encyclopaedia entry and decide why the writer has used two tenses. Explain your findings by writing down and completing the following statement:

> *The writer uses the present tense when he is writing about* _____ _____ *but switches to the past tense when he is writing about* _____ _____ .

Text

Colloquial English includes vocabulary and expressions which are closer to everyday, informal speech.

Colloquial English can include the use of slang, shortened words with the apostrophe (see page 22) and ellipsis (see page 40).

1 Slang is the name given to a set of colloquial words and phrases not normally used in formal standard English:

> *mate, taking the mick*

Find and write down three examples of slang from the diary. Then write the same word or phrase in standard English. Here is one to get you started:

> *a place name that sticks out like a sore thumb*   slang
>
> *a place name which is clearly different from others*   standard English

2 Find and write down four examples of where the writer has shortened words using the apostrophe. Then write the words in full. Reread the extract, using the full version instead of the shortened one. What difference does this make to the extract?

Write a sentence or two to explain what difference this makes to the text.

3 How many of these words describe the tone of the diary text?

- friendly
- cold
- distant
- inviting
- patronising
- informative
- persuasive
- personal

4 What do you think the writer of the diary text was trying to achieve when he wrote it?

A **fact** is a piece of information which can be proved to be true.

The encyclopaedia text is concerned with facts:

> It has an area of 276 miles.

This piece of information can be proved by measuring it.

An **opinion** is a belief held by someone which cannot be proved.

The diary text mixes fact and opinion:

> ...the magnificent stone castle...

The castle is certainly built of stone – this is a fact that can be checked. The word *magnificent* is the opinion of the writer.

5 Draw two columns and head them **Fact** and **Opinion**.

Find these phrases and sentences in the texts and write the quotations in the correct column.

- *Edward drove out the local people...*
- *The décor is purple and white...*
- *It's a magical place...*
- *Many kinds of sea birds are found on the rocky coast.*
- *...lots of brass and copper hanging on the walls.*
- *something limp, lacklustre and totally devoid of imagination*
- *Holyhead has a regular passenger service to Ireland.*
- *Beaumaris is the county town.*
- *The climate is drier than the rest of Wales.*
- *Top nosh!*

6 Write a paragraph to explain which of the two texts you find more interesting. Include quotations from the extracts which support your viewpoint.

5 ▷ Planning your own writing

Write two descriptions of a place you know well. One should be a
formal and factual account; the other should be a personal account
which is lively and informal. Your audience will know nothing about
the place you are describing and your job is to inform them and,
in your personal account, to entertain and persuade them.

▷▷ STARTING POINT

- Choose a place you know well –
  your town or village, your school, a
  building you know, a sporting
  venue, or a concert hall.

- Research any interesting facts about
  the place.

- Make notes on any historical or
  geographical features of the place.

- Make notes about the last time you
  visited it.

▷▷ CLUES FOR SUCCESS

- Plan both pieces carefully, jotting
  down the details you want to
  include.

- Attempt the factual account first
  using the encyclopaedia entry as
  a model.

- Plan two paragraphs, one dealing
  with the past and one with the
  present. Vary your verb tenses to
  suit your writing.

- For the second piece, break your
  writing into paragraphs or use
  sub-headings.

- Use the present tense to give a
  feeling of immediacy.

- Use rhetorical questions to connect
  to your reader.

- Remember to mix fact with opinion
  and to use features of colloquial
  English.

WRITING FRAMES

You may find the following writing frames helpful.

Factual account

Place name	Give the name of the town.
Geographical detail	*This town is situated in... It has...* *The climate is...* *Travel to and from... is...*
Historical detail	*The place was originally... Later it...*
Other information	*Currently the place is...*

Personal account

Paragraph and contents	**Example**
Arrival. Introduce the piece and give your impression of the place.	*I'm here!... The first things I notice are...*
Give some facts about the place.	*We set off for... It used to be...*
First activity and some detail or history of the feature you are describing.	*It looks...*
Main activity or feature. Give a detailed account of what you are doing and what it is like.	*Now comes the best part of my visit...*
Conclusion. Give your feelings about the place.	*Finally, it's time to go home. I feel...*

 **REDRAFTING AND IMPROVING**

- Have you used some interesting and appropriate facts?

- Have you used standard English for your formal, factual account?

- Have you checked for accurate grammar, spelling and punctuation?

- Check that you have used a more colloquial style for your informal writing, including using the apostrophe for shortening words, slang and ellipsis.

- Does your second piece make use of the present tense?

- Have you used rhetorical questions to connect with your reader?

- Make sure that you have included your feelings and reactions to the place.

- Check that your punctuation and spelling are correct.

6 Looking back

- Writers can use **colloquial English** when aiming to entertain or persuade readers.

- **Rhetorical questions** are used to involve the reader.

- Writers vary the **tense of verbs** to suit their material.

- Information texts make use of **facts**; persuasive texts mix **facts** and **opinion**.

Glossary

Active In the active form of a verb, the subject carries out an action.

Adverb A word which can give more information about a verb.

Alliteration The repetition of initial consonant sounds to create an effect.

Chronology The arrangement of events in the order in which they happened.

Contrast A clear and striking difference between two things.

Ellipsis The omission of words or phrases.

Etymology The history of a particular word.

Euphemism A way of saying an unpleasant or offensive thing in a mild or pleasant way.

First person Writing can be in the first person (using *I* or *we*), the second person (*you*) or the third person (*she*, *he*, *they*).

Image A vivid picture in words created by a writer to help us to imagine what is being described.

Imperatives Forms of verbs which command, ask or invite the reader to do something.

Metaphor A way of comparing things without using the words *like* or *as*, where the writer writes about something as if it really were something else.

Mnemonic A way of helping you to remember something.

Passive In the passive form of a verb, the subject is on the receiving end of the action.

Personification A special kind of metaphor in which things and ideas are spoken about as if they were people.

Prefix A group of letters added to the start of a word to change its meaning or to create a new word.

Sensory Where a writer refers to the five senses of sight, hearing, smell, taste and language touch. Writers use the senses to develop and strengthen their descriptions.

Silent letters Letters which are not sounded when the word is spoken.

Simile A way of comparing things in an unusual way, so that the writer creates an image in the reader's mind. A simile uses the words *like* or *as*.

Structure The structure of a text is the way it is put together in paragraphs.

Suffix A letter or group of letters added to the end of a word to change its meaning or to create a new word.

Syntax The study of sentence structures – the way words are used together in a sentence.

Tense The form of the verb which shows when something happened – either the present, the past or the future.